The Boy from the Bl...

By Ken Ju...

Contents

Foreword

Chapter 1: Life in Queen Victoria's beautiful country

Chapter 2: The Eleven Plus and Grammar School

Chapter 3: Church and Social Life

Chapter 4: Adolescence

Chapter 5: University Student Life

Chapter 6: Transition to an Academic's Life

Chapter 7: Northern Ireland 1969-72

Chapter 8: A Year at the University of Illinois

Chapter 9: Queen's and the Continuing Troubles

Chapter 10: Sheffield and British Steel

Chapter 11: Back to Academia

About the Author

Foreword

The initial motivation for this book was to describe social life in the industrial working class just after World War II and to illustrate the move from the working class into the middle class, and even a brush with Royalty. It gradually became apparent that it was best to write a form of partial autobiography covering not only the transition from working class to middle class but also deep experience of the height of the Troubles in Northern Ireland, a secondment to the USA at the time of Watergate, and the move from "old" university life to "new" university life. Very few of the characters in this story have been given fictional names. Any factual errors are entirely the fault of the author.

In memory of Keith

© **Ken Jukes, January 2018**

Chapter 1 Life in Queen Victoria's beautiful country

The fog was thickening as Ken walked towards the railway bridge, passing the gloomy factories that clanged to the sound of the beating of red hot metal. This was the Black Country, an area in the English Midlands that made everything from nails to bridges and railway engines. The industrial sprawl, smoke and grime was so marked that it is said that Queen Victoria ordered the curtains on the carriage of her royal train to be pulled as she passed through Tipton on the main line from London to Birmingham to Glasgow.

Ken arrived at his terraced house and walked through the entry, a passageway for each pair of houses leading through to their back doors. The house had a small private front garden bounded by brick walls on two sides and a hedge at the front. The front door opened into the so-called front room which was kept for "best" being normally only used on a Sunday and at party times.

"Back already," said his mother Hilda tenderly, as she prepared the beef stew, holding David in her arms, whilst the other children Margaret, Keith, Roger and Norma huddled around the coke fire which glowed in the cast iron blackened grate. "Yes mom," said Ken, his mind still being on the fog and how it had ruined the chance of football with the Denbigh Estate gang on the dirt pitch. Perhaps it would be clear enough for him soon to join a game against the lamp-post in the street. "I'm afraid that Clive has brushed the gas mantle again with his head and broken it, so take this florin Ken, and pop over to White's shop to get a new one so we can see in here. Get a pound of sugar at the same time. Off you go now." "Why me again?" said Ken, quickly evading the attempted friendly cuff round the ear, but off he went. White's lay in a row of five small terraced shops alongside the Tavern on the main road from Dudley to West Bromwich. The owners of each shop lived in the back or upstairs rooms and served in the shop. "A new gas mantle and a pound of margarine please," said Ken to Mrs White. She put the margarine on the counter and got out a pair of step ladders to reach the mantles which were kept on the fourth wooden shelf behind a glass door.

3

"That will be one and tuppence," said Mrs White, Ken handing over the florin and getting 10 pence back in change.

"There you are mom," said Ken as he returned within 15 minutes through the fog. "Not again!" said Hilda in frustration, "I asked you to get a pound of sugar and so why have you brought a pound of margarine?" Although Ken was regarded as quite bright, it was a mystery to Hilda why he often came back with the wrong items. Not that Ken himself understood why. "Put the gas mantle on the light fitting, Keith, but do take care, it is very fragile." Keith, the second eldest of the five boys, climbed onto a chair and carefully replaced the mantle, the children cheering when the gas was turned on and the sickly yellow light lit up the room, enhancing the limited light from the coke fire. In the meantime, Ken went off again to exchange the margarine for sugar.

Hilda muttered to herself about her husband Reginald. No doubt he had finished at the gasworks and was enjoying a few pints in the Tavern. "How did I get into this?" she said to herself as the stew started to boil on the gas cooker. Hilda now had seven children.

Her own family was relatively affluent and were against her marriage to Reg in 1938, seeing it as being below her station in life. Nevertheless she was in love with Reg, one of six children himself and a fitter at the Tipton gas works. He had figured very highly in the county in the School Certificate examinations and it was rumoured would have been able to progress to Oxford University. However, the concepts of University and sixth form (grades 11 and 12) were totally alien to the working-class families of Tipton, a town of some 35,000 in the heart of the Black Country. University education just did not figure in one's aspirations, being for posh people. Many of the schoolteachers in the local Grammar and Secondary School had been to two-year training colleges, those with a university background flaunting their ermine and brightly coloured robes at the annual Speech Days. Reg had followed in the footsteps of many of the local generation, leaving high school at the age of 15 and taking a 5-year apprenticeship in a nearby factory. His had been at the local gas works, which produced town gas from coal, the process producing coke as a bi-product, a cheaper domestic alternative to coal.

After tucking into the stew, Ken and Roger wandered out into the fog but it was now so thick that one could only see about 5 yards. Waiting there were their friends Alan and Derek, who were always ready to play, their favourite games being football and marbles. The gas lamp in the street was just visible from the pavement, its eerie light complementing the muffled sounds of passers-by. Goals in the 2-a-side game were scored by hitting the lamp-post, making the strategy between defending close to the post, or attacking, quite an art. Traffic was normally very light off the main roads and almost non-existent in the fog, the greatest danger being from passing cyclists who might suddenly emerge from the fog. Only a year ago, Ken had suffered a broken collar-bone from such an incident, the workman on the bike disappearing over the handlebars, swearing at Ken as he flew through the air. The boys' heavy leather ball soon got lost in the thick fog. "Let's go back in," said Roger, the fourth of Hilda's five boys and so the boys returned to their homes, gathering around the fire and toasting stale bread on a fork held against the bars of the coke fire. The family were so grateful to their next door neighbour Mrs Parker, who had just one child, Joyce, and who kindly saved the crusts from her loaves to give to Hilda's family. Ken was sure Mr Parker was not aware of this; he always seemed to be miserable, finding it difficult to live next door to the large and rather noisy Jukes family.

Electricity would be some years before coming to the household. It was hard to read in the dim gas lighting; indeed as the boys grew in height the gas mantle continued to be broken on a regular basis, reducing the family on many occasions to the use of candles and paraffin lamps. Town gas was used for cooking and lighting as well as for a gas poker, this producing a friendly flame for slowly igniting the coal and coke fires in the two rooms downstairs. The rear room served as a living room, a dining room, a kitchen, and, on Fridays, a bathroom. The two-up two-down house did have the relative luxury of a gas fire in the main bedroom. There was no running water in the house, so buckets for potties were in constant use, whilst Fridays saw a tin bath brought in and placed before the fire. The toilets were some distance up the yard, past the brick built wash-house and the dilapidated coal shed. It was rare to see toilet paper, newspaper being used regularly and occasionally glossy magazine paper which had an unfortunate tendency to block the toilet causing it to overflow and to need to be cleaned out. With so many having to use the toilet, the Jukes boys used to dash across the shared back garden to use Mrs Parker's toilet in an emergency.

Inside the wash-house was a large white ceramic sink where men also shaved. Alongside the sink was a boiler with gas heating for washing day, always a Monday in the community. The mangle was a god-send, even though the handle for turning the rollers was hard work, especially when putting sheets through. Ken always wondered why many people called their wash-house the "bruce", not realizing the use of "bruce" as slang for "brew house". Washing was taken in a basket to a rope line in the back garden, the drying washing being soiled with black particles from steam engines that passed through the railway cutting at the top of the garden. The cutting was deep and grassy, the engines belching out their steam and smoke as they moved from Great Bridge to Dudley.

Clive, the eldest of the children, had now returned from his evening paper-round and Margaret had got back from the rehearsal for the variety show given by players from the local Methodist church. "Let's play the word game," said Ken, as competitive as ever, as the children huddled around the glowing coke fire, eying the toast. The Jukes family relished the hot toast covered with lashings of butter. The children had developed a range of mental games. In the word game one person chose a letter and then this was passed round to add other letters, always keeping in mind one's word had to be declared if challenged. You each had three lives, losing a life if your word was in error when challenged, or if you were forced to add the last letter. It was Ken's turn to start another round with Keith, Roger, Clive and Norma. "z," said Ken, "e," said Keith, "b," said Roger, "r," said Clive, "a," said Norma. Ken was furious; "How could I be so stupid?" he thought, realizing he could only add an s, so ending the word and losing his last life. "Let's play again," he said. Ken

6

was regarded as a terrible loser; he didn't like losing but he was never knocked down, being always ready to battle again to try and win.

After losing three times, Ken was ready to change tack. This time they moved to the game of lists, sorting out the pencils and paper and moving across the room to where the gaslight enabled them to see more clearly. Keith kicked off by saying "you have one minute to write down all capital cities beginning with the letter B." Lists of names, flowers, animals, rivers and towns were normally amongst their favourites. At the end of the round each list was taken in turn and you only scored a point for an entry in your list if that entry did not appear in anyone else's list. Ken lost again but decided to retreat upstairs to read his comics in the dim paraffin-lamp light in the bedroom.

Ken jumped into bed with a "brrrr"; after all it was November and the fog outside seemed to cool the house dramatically. After a few minutes reading a Kit Carson comic, he pulled the sheet over his head to keep warm. It was his turn to sleep at the bottom, the bed being shared with Keith and Roger who slept at the top. Ken heard the muffled whistle of the double header goods train as it went under the bridge at Lower Church Lane and entered the cutting at the rear of the garden. The steam engines puffed and panted, one at the front and one at the rear of the train, the rumbling of the wagons rattling the window frames. Ken was an enthusiastic train-spotter and liked the excitement in the dryness of the summer when the banks were regularly set on fire by sparks from the steam engines. The boys would then join with neighbours, taking off their jackets and pullovers and using them to beat out the flames.

The railway behind the garden was fondly called the low-level, and passed through another tunnel underneath the main line at Dudley Port station. The low-level was used mainly for goods trains by the London, Midland and Scottish Railways (the LMS) and the Great Western Railways (GWR). The LMS and GWR shared the low-level line, the GWR also running a wedge-shaped passenger diesel coach train from Dudley station to Birmingham Snow Hill station. Ken felt that the low-level engines and diesel lacked glamour, much preferring the named LMS engines like "The Royal Scot", "Silver Jubilee" and the Patriot Class as well as GWR's Kings, Castles, Halls and Manors. Neither the LMS nor the GWR steam engines usually included a named engine on the low-level line, so it was a great thrill when one did go past, usually an LMS train being diverted to the Bescot railway yards at Walsall. Ken smiled to himself, thinking how neat it was that lbw could stand for London-Birmingham-Wolverhampton and not just leg-before-wicket, as in the game of cricket. As the engines on the main line passed the signal box just north of the station, he could read their numbers using the binoculars loaned to them by their Uncle Arthur, who had procured them in the war from the body of a German soldier. Beyond the main line one could see quite clearly the battlements of Dudley Castle, defiantly standing on a hill overlooking the Black Country, but ruined by the cannons of Oliver Cromwell in the battles between the Royalists and Roundheads.

Ken's love of steam engines was fostered further through his Sunday morning trip to the Tipton gas works, when he took his father's breakfast there, usually a bacon and egg sandwich with lashings of hot brown sauce, all wrapped in greaseproof paper and newspaper. The production of gas from coal generated large amounts of slack (fine grained coal waste) as well as coke, and the works maintained a set of industrial steam engines to move the fuels and waste around the site. "Come on lad," said Mr Wilson one Sunday. "I'm just off to move the wagons of slack, so jump in and you can have a go at driving the engine." "Great and ta very much," said Ken as he clambered aboard the "George Diamond", a small tank engine. "There you are lad, give that a pull." Ken was thrilled as he pulled the whistle chain, creating a deafening shrill sound as steam shot into the air. "What's that for Mr Wilson?" said Ken, pointing at a long rod. "That starts the engine," said Mr Wilson as he moved the long lever and the engine roared into action, the wheels momentarily skidding on the tracks. Ken was allowed to move the lever himself, the engine gradually picking up speed and moving round a bend towards the mountains of slack. "Wow, I'd like to be a train driver when I grow up," said Ken to Mr Wilson, who nodded wisely, realizing that this was a common reaction of small boys. Soon they were in amongst the mountains of slack, changing the points, hooking up the wagons and moving them to a siding where they would be picked up by a main line locomotive.

Ken suddenly awoke to shouts from his mother. It was cold, dark and misty outside and everyone jumped quickly out of bed as smoke poured up the stairwell towards the two bedrooms. "Get in here near the window," cried Hilda, "Hurry." Reg had arrived back from the Tavern in a state of drunkenness, had quarrelled with Hilda as usual, and had stayed downstairs smoking his "Players" cigarettes, whilst the rest of the family were in bed. As he slumbered, his cigarette fell from his mouth into the fabric of the chair. Not noticing, he gathered himself and heaved his way up the narrow winding wooden staircase to the bedroom. Now he was downstairs fighting flames in the rear room as the children and their mother gathered at the bedroom window adjacent to the street. Buckets of water were poured into the blaze as Reg moved quickly back and forth to the tap in the adjacent wash-house. The commotion alerted neighbours who started to appear from the mist and called for the two youngest children to be dropped from the bedroom window. The fire engine seemed to take an eternity to arrive but when it did, Reg had the fire under control.

Following the clear-up, the daylight slowly emerged through the mist and neighbours brought along bread, porridge oats, and two cups of sugar. The milkman made his daily delivery and soon empty stomachs were satisfied. The Council man came round and organized emergency clothing for Ken and Roger, all of whose clothes had disappeared in the fire. It was very exciting, the lack of clothing meaning a half-day off school for the two boys.

It was about this time that Ken experienced his first sexual encounter but he did not know this at the time. The event centred on a comic fair organized by one of the posher lads from the street, Peter Milner, the comics being laid out on tables in a large tent in Peter's garden. There were about ten boys in the tent and they were all asked to take their "willies" out and move the foreskin back and forth. "Odd," thought Ken, not realizing until several years later what it was all about.

Saturday morning came and Ken and Roger worked on their trolley. Their contraption had a wooden seat, about four foot long and eighteen inches wide, the seat lying across two spindles located at the front and rear. The wheels and spindles for the trolley had been recovered as usual from two worn-out prams, these having been found on wasteland alongside the derelict school near the railway station. A steering rope was fastened to either side of the front spindle of the trolley and, by pulling on one side, the rope allowed the spindle to be turned, giving control over the direction of the trolley. The rear wheels were of greater diameter than the front ones and a wooden block with a small lever had been fitted alongside the rim of the right-side big wheel, giving a form of brake that generally was quite useless. "Good, am yow ready yet," said their friend Derek in his best Black Country accent, as he and another friend, Alan, came up the street pulling their trolleys behind them. "Yes," said Roger, "we will start up near the gas works at the canal bridge, come down from the canal bridge along Station Road and then onto Park Lane East, turn left over the railway bridge and down the hill, and go past our house towards Lower Church Lane. The winner is the one who gets the furthest. Ken, you stop at the junction with Park Lane and wave us when the road is clear." So off they went making run after run, with the boys taking it in turns to be the lookout. The scarcity of traffic in the early fifties, coupled with factories usually closing after the one o'clock bull, or siren, meant that the roads were very quiet.

"Alan, can you help us change this wheel," said Roger as Derek moved off again, pulling his trolley up the railway bridge and towards the gas works. A few minutes passed as a lorry, carrying steaming coke from the gas works, turned into Park Lane East and trundled down the hill. "Yahoo," shouted Derek as the lorry passed the three boys, Derek standing up on his trolley with his hands holding his guide rope and clinging to a bar at the rear of the lorry. As the lorry braked at the junction with Lower Church Lane, Derek's trolley carried on underneath the rear wheels leaving him sprawling and banging his face against the rear of the lorry, knocking out his two front teeth and grazing his elbows and knees as he fell to the floor. "What an idiot," shouted Ken as they picked Derek up in the road and surveyed his slightly mangled trolley, the lorry driver swearing and shouting at them.

Next day saw the boys all attending Sunday school, after which they gathered in Ken's back garden for a game of marbles, playing with "pretties", these being small glass marbles with streaks of colouring in the glass. All the boys hated iron marbles, no-one daring to try and exchange these or even to bring any of them along. Ken had a tin with about 30 marbles in, Roger about 40, Alan 60 and Derek 56. They first played the game of chucka. " Giz a chucka 3," said Ken to Alan who agreed and passed three pretties to Ken. The others looked on as Ken put three of his marbles with the three of Alan's, crouched and threw the marbles from a line in the dirt to a small hole, about 4 inches in diameter and about 6 feet away. The boys all rushed to the hole, which had two marbles in; "yes, I win," yelled Ken, gathering all six into his hand and stuffing them into his trouser pocket. The game of chucka is based on winning if you get an even number of marbles in the hole, losing if an odd number go in, with your opponent throwing again if you land no marbles in the hole. The game went on for almost two hours, Roger and Derek eventually being miffed at losing all their marbles and Alan and Ken battling on. Tensions always became very high when chuckas as large as a chucka 20, say, were challenged and accepted, a huge scramble occurring to check how many were in the hole. Arguments about how many were in were heated and very common, it not being unknown for one of the parties to drop a marble quietly onto the ground, hoping no-one else noticed. Another issue was that Alan could not be allowed to lose all his marbles, since this inevitably led to him going home in tears. His mother would then come storming down to Ken's house demanding all his marbles be given back.

"Let's play Killer," said Roger, Ken lending him four marbles. Derek exchanged a toffee for two marbles and away the four boys went. This time the players threw a marble in turn. If they entered the target hole they got an extra throw and moved on to the next hole. An extra throw was also generated by hitting a competitor's marble. After getting into each of the four holes, their marble became a "killer marble". Having become killer, you then threw your marble to try and hit an opponent's marble, which you then won, excluding the owner from the game. The game continued until only one competitor was left in the game. Many hours were spent playing Killer, a tactical cat and mouse situation following, when more than one of the boys held killer marbles simultaneously.

After an hour of Killer, Ken suggested a new game in which each of the boys placed the same number of marbles in a circle drawn in the dirt with a twig. A line was then drawn two paces from the circle. It was agreed that turns would be taken starting with the youngest, the idea being to throw underarm one of your own marbles at the circle and then pick up any marbles dislodged from the circle. The winner was the one with the greatest number of marbles once the circle became empty. The game was not very popular with the boys.

"Enough of marbles," said Keith joining the boys. "Let's play duckstool. Here is a full-size brick, now get your ducks." Each boy searched the garden for a fair sized stone or broken brick, as big as their hands would hold. "I'll be on guard first," said Keith, marking out a line in the dirt about 10 feet from the upright full brick, Keith having placed his own duck on top. The idea was that each boy threw their duck in turn at the duckstool (the upright full brick) and if they knocked it over they tried to retrieve their duck and get back behind the line before being tagged by Keith. If you were tagged you took over guard of the duckstool, Keith then becoming one of the throwers. If they failed to knock over the duckstool, they waited by their duck and tried to pick it up and knock Keith's off with their own duck still in their hand and run back to the line, all before being tagged by Keith. So if all missed, then it became very tense as Keith eyed them all and tagged anyone who touched their duck before they could knock off his own.

The weekdays dragged slowly from Monday onwards, being dominated by attending the Church primary school followed by football or cricket in the evenings on a piece of wasteland alongside the railway station; then tea and finally street games. When the boys had lost all their marbles to friends from other streets, they would resort to collecting odd buttons and playing each other for these. A chalk line was placed 10 feet from the edge of a wall and you each threw one button towards the wall, the winner being the one whose button finished nearest the wall. Whilst the game whiled away the time, the boys never had much enthusiasm for winning buttons and would soon change tack, often ending up alongside the canal, digging for worms and catching small sticklebacks using string or cotton thread as a line.

Drama occurred one afternoon, when Ken and Roger disobeyed Hilda by going fishing rather than staying at home. All went quiet until Roger suddenly fell into the dark murky waters of the canal. Neither he nor Ken could swim, Ken shouting "float, float" and then rushing away for help. Roger was incredibly lucky in that a Mr Howes was nearby, and dived in and rescued him. Ken felt guilty for years about the incident. Did Roger slip or trip, or what happened?

Swimming was in fact quite a passion for members of the family and people of the town, the local swimming baths providing many hours of enjoyment. Clive, Margaret and Keith were all good swimmers and it all looked very easy to Ken and Roger. So there they were in a long line with Keith, waiting for entry. Sessions took place in 30 minute intervals, and one might have to wait up to 90 minutes to get into the baths. Eventually they were in and changed in the small cubicles alongside the pool. Ken and Roger were full of bravado, and with a short run jumped into the water in the shallow end. Glug, glug,glug….., Ken recalled as he and Roger went under, surfaced and somehow scrambled out of the pool. It would be some two years before they learned to swim and dared to jump in again! After swimming, the boys would call into the bakers opposite the swimming baths. Swimming made them ravenous and they would use any money they had to purchase one or more half loaves. These they devoured as they walked back along the canal footpath towards home. There is nothing like freshly made bread after swimming!

Another of Ken's passions was cricket, he and the family enjoying the occasional coach ride to watch his father Reg captain the Gas Works team against other teams in the area. The part of the yard at the rear of the house that ran alongside the washhouse and coal bunker, had a high boundary wall separating it from the Parker's yard. A dustbin lid formed the wickets and was placed upright against the step leading into the back garden. The ball was usually a tennis ball but sometimes a cork ball was available. Bowling was always underarm and great efforts were made to spin the ball. A direct hit into the alleyway scored two, a hit against the wall or backdoor behind the bowler scored one. The rules also allowed the batsman to hit right over the top of the houses into the street, but the roof was very high and going over it was rare, very difficult and attracted 12 runs! You were out if caught, including a one-handed catch after the ball hit the boundary wall with the Parker's or caught one handed if the ball came back off the high roof. No running was required of the batsman. Scores tended to be quite high, with a batsman sometimes scoring a century.

The Parkers were very understanding when the ball went into their property but this was not the case with the other two neighbours, the Gayles and the Prices. Mrs Gayle would get particularly angry if the boys tried to recover a ball from her garden. She would run out of her house shouting "Bagger orff you bladdy baggers."

The yard just outside the back door of Ken's house was completely enclosed and permitted plenty of practice in kicking a ball against the far wall. Football was very popular, the wasteland alongside the Territorial Army shed and low level railway being extensively used. With the number of players on each side being so great and the dirt pitch so small, it was quite impossible to develop skills of passing or dribbling, most games seeing boys from around the area crowded around the ball and chasing it like wasps around jam.

The land there also provided a venue for cricket in the summer, proper wickets (stumps), bats and a cork ball being used. A rough uneven dirt wicket was not a good place to learn to bat, especially against the fast bowling of the older boys of the area. Ken had the knack of standing away from the stumps and playing the ball at the last moment. This infuriated the older boys who would say "Yove got more jam than Hartleys!" This led to Ken having the knickname "Jamma". Little was he to know that it would follow him all the way through Grammar School, with Roger being called Jamma Junior and youngest brother David initially being called Marma (derived from marmalade!). Indeed, on Ken's departure from the Grammar School, Roger was elevated to "Jamma" and David to "Jamma Junior" and eventually to "Jamma".

Chapter 2 The Eleven-Plus and Grammar School

Ken was now in his final year at St Martin's, the Church primary school. He had shown himself to be one of the brightest boys in the class and was placed in the top row of just 6 students who sat in pairs. His main rival was Henry, both being particularly strong at mathematics. The other 42 students sat in six single file rows of 7 students each, students moving between rows over time according to how their teacher felt they were progressing in the regular quizzes. "Now boys," said Mr Worthington, "we are going to do a practice test tomorrow for entry to the Grammar School. Should you be selected after the real exam, it is likely you will go to Tipton Grammar, but we occasionally have boys and girls who pass and attend Dudley Grammar or even Wednesbury High School." Ken was fully aware of this, his Uncle Ted having attended the latter and was now an established Journalist. Ken was worried about Dudley Grammar since Keith, a real genius in the Arts and General Knowledge, had passed for Dudley the previous year but was very unhappy there. The trouble was that Hilda could not afford the quality of uniform that children at Dudley Grammar wore, and Keith was continually being bullied both because of his clothing and also due to coming from a large and poor family.

So the big day arrived and Ken made his way to Park Lane Secondary School where the 11-plus exam was to be administered by a tough but kindly teacher named Mr Titley. All seemed to go well with the exam, there being a huge booklet of questions covering both Mathematics and English.

"Ken," said Hilda on his return, "you know that Clive is starting his new job as a trainee journalist in the summer. I want you now to take over his paper-round, starting on Monday. I have spoken to Mr Martin about it and both he and Mrs Martin are happy about you taking over. You can accompany Clive for a week and then Mr Martin will write the house numbers on the top of the papers so you should soon pick it up. You will need to get up earlier than you do now, be there for seven in the morning and straight after school in the evening. The evening round is much longer than the morning

16

round and goes right down into Tame Road, before returning on the opposite side of Horseley Heath and then repeating the morning round up Park Lane East and Station Road, Howard Street, Keeling Street, and back down Lower Church Lane." "Yes mom," said Ken who had received the customary one shilling per week pocket money on his tenth birthday. "Will I still be able to keep the tips when I collect paper money on Saturdays?" "Of course," said Hilda, the epitome of kindness and fairness, "but you will of course hand the ten shillings wages to me each week." "Yipee," said Ken, excited at the possibility of his new found wealth.

And so it came to pass. Ken would collect his papers in a canvas bag and run from house to house in the mornings. The evenings were a totally different proposition, Ken being weighed down with not one, but two heavy bags of papers and magazines. "Why do women read these magazines," he thought, "The Woman, Women's Own, Women's World, baahh." Whilst he could complete the morning round in forty minutes, it took up to two hours in the evening. The saving grace was a call at Granny's home in Howard Street in the evening, a hot cup of tea or a bottle of orange juice always being on offer. The tea was always boiling hot but he drank it without hesitation. "Yo'm a real asbestos guts," said Granny, in her thick Black Country accent. "Dow yo call im nerms," Grandad would say to her. "Yo shut it, yo owd fool," Grandma would reply. "Ken, pop over to the off-licence and get us a jug of stout." "Of course Granny," this being one of his regular chores.

Ken collected the paper money on Saturdays, keeping records in his account book. Whilst most families paid on time, there were a number for whom cigarettes, beer and food came before paying for papers. Often they would pay a small contribution, avoiding the debt getting too large. Mr Martin never questioned this, paying on the never-never seemed to be a way of life in the area.

The saddest case was Rachel, a lady who lived alone in a detached house at the rear of the back-to-back houses, her home bordering the edge of the canal. Rachel's windows were all broken; there were no curtains downstairs, no carpet on the red-tiled floor and no sign of furniture apart from a dilapidated and torn sofa. It was rumoured that Rachel's family had emigrated to Canada, leaving her behind, so that she now existed alone on the minimum state pension and continued to suffer mental problems, talking and shouting to herself. She was however a lady of immense pride and each week Ken felt a terrible pang of guilt as Rachel paid her paper money and gave him a one penny tip. It would certainly have hurt Rachel's feelings to refuse the tip. Her sense of pride and independence was exemplified by her method of securing coal to keep her warm. From time to time she would venture to the canal wharf, where barges unloaded their coal. Rachel carried two tin buckets, filling them and then walking the half mile back to her home. She walked in the centre of the road, taking one bucket forward some 20 yards at a time. Although neighbours were always helping each other, no-one dared interfere with Rachel's method, everyone being sensitive to her pride and independence.

Moving along to Keeling Street, Ken marvelled at the wealth of Mr and Mrs Follows, a couple without any airs or graces, who ran a coal merchants business and clearly made a significant income. They dressed well and owned cars and televisions well before any of their neighbours. They were always generous with their tipping and also followed closely Ken's school successes.

Further down the road was Mrs Woodhouse, who was a model of kindness, tipping Ken well each week and again encouraging him with his schoolwork. Opposite Mrs Woodhouse lived the Richards family, whose home was directly opposite Ken's back garden, on the other side of the railway cutting. Keith had an air rifle and would shoot at targets in the back garden, but sometimes he and Ken would fire at small sparrows on the roof of the Richards' house. The Richards family seemed to be extremely wealthy, their daughter even taking delivery of the Lancet, a magazine for doctors. Ken wondered each time when he collected the paper money whether they would mention the air rifle, but they never did. One family in very poor dilapidated housing in Lower Church Lane, the Harpers, seemed to be particularly poor, the father always in and out of prison and the boys constantly in trouble with the police. Mrs Harper was a very proud woman however and she never fell behind with their paper bill.

Besides having the responsibility of collecting and handling the paper money, Ken and Henry had a joint responsibility at St Martin's School of taking the weekly savings collection to be deposited in the General Post Office (GPO), this involving walking along the canal footpath and then down a hill, a total distance of about a mile. On the opposite bank of the canal stood an iron works, the labourers catching and throwing rods of red hot steel along the side of the works using clippers about a yard long. It all seemed very dangerous but one never heard of accidents there. The boys were usually fortunate enough to be able to purchase two pennyworth of Pontefract cakes, made from black liquorice on the way to the GPO.

The big day came before Ken's 11th birthday, his School announcing that twelve of the class of forty-eight had passed the Eleven-Plus exam, all being offered places at Tipton Grammar School. Auntie Dot and her husband Uncle Ted were amazingly generous, giving Ken a ten shilling note to purchase a second-hand bicycle from his friend Henry. Sadly however, Henry's parents were not in favour of the Grammar School, had no money for a school uniform, and Henry was unable to take his place, going instead to Park Lane, the non-academic secondary modern school.

Uncle Ted and Reg had a wicked sense of humour, making life difficult for Margaret and Joyce and their current boyfriends, each of whom they eventually married. Passing through the entry one day and finding Joyce cuddling with her steady boyfriend Bill, Ted said "Hello Joyce, who is this then? He's not the same chap you were with last night." Fortunately Bill had been with Joyce and so trouble was averted. On another occasion, Margaret was with her steady boyfriend Tony, Reg saying "and what size shoe do you take?" Tony had small feet and took a size 7. "That's no bloody good here," said Reg, we all have feet bigger than that so we can't look to you for hand me downs." Tony thought "silly bugger," but was not deterred. Indeed on his first official visit to Margaret's home, Ken and Roger had repainted the front door a bright blue but with cheap industrial paint that never seemed to dry. Tony had unfortunately arrived in his suit and leaned against the door post as he came in, ruining his jacket!

Life at the Grammar School began on September 5th, Ken walking on his own along Lower Church Lane to Alexandra Road, a distance of some two miles. He was attired in short grey flannel trousers, a black blazer with a school badge made of fabric and sewn into the left hand breast, and a cap, also sporting a school badge, this one made of metal. On his back he carried a small empty leather satchel, purchased by Hilda at the market place in nearby Great Bridge. Elder brother Clive had now left the Grammar School and had embarked on his career as a journalist so Ken felt very nervous about what lay before him. He had heard rumours about the rough treatment meted out to new students at Park Lane and wondered what happened at the Grammar, especially since things had just changed dramatically there, the Grammar now being co-educational.

School began with an assembly in the main hall, the headmaster Mr G. S. Smith wearing a black academic gown and speaking with a cultured, stern voice. His Deputy was the former Head of the Girls' Grammar School, a spinster named Miss Farrington, who seemed less stern, but like Mr Smith, she seemed to have no sense of humour. Ken found himself allocated to form 1A and later discovered that this was the top form, the others being named 1B and 1C, each containing about 30 pupils. Classes whizzed by and soon it came to the lunch hour, Ken running home to tell Hilda all about his morning. After a cheese sandwich and a cup of tea, he ran back to school, the afternoon passing quickly and school ending at 4:00 p.m. He crossed the road and started along a rough dirt track that ran between two mounds of coal slack, these now being overgrown with tall grass and weeds. "Ow," he cried as he was hit on the side with what turned into a shower of small bricks and pebbles, thrown by two second year boys. Avoidance of their trap became a regular occurrence, forcing Ken to take longer routes or ambling and then suddenly spurting passed the assailants.

Bullying was a regular feature of school life and was made more difficult by teasing about holes in Ken's shoes, no underpants, and a lack of hankies. On one occasion, he was chased by a group of more affluent students who chanted "show us your handkerchief." He quickly turned the lining of his inside pocket towards the bullies, none of them realizing they had been tricked. The problem of holes in the soles of shoes was a recurring one. Ken, Roger and later David were forever vying with each other to get hold of cereal packets such as Corn Flakes and Puffed Wheat, the cardboard then being cut to shape and inserted in two layers into the shoe, covering the hole. Unfortunately, wet weather made the cardboard mushy and the feet wet. Even more embarrassing was when on several occasions the sole of Ken's shoe became unstuck and flapped as he walked along, a perfect excuse for even more teasing and bullying.

Besides doing relatively well academically, coming in the top 14 of the class, Ken gained some admiration due to his success in the school cross-country. He was of course used to running paper rounds in the mornings and evenings, the latter carrying two heavy bags, and so it was no surprise that he won the races very easily for the next three years. In the very first race he finished four minutes ahead of the boy in second place, David Dugmore, who crossed the finishing line and immediately spewed up on the floor of the boys' changing room. It was during March that first year, that Ken was again leading the cross country and was turning into Alexandra Road at the traffic roundabout near the School. An ambulance passed by into Lower Church Lane, Hilda waving at Ken through the side window. It transpired she was on her way home with the latest arrival to the family, Dawn, the eighth sibling.

Another highlight of Ken's first year was the annual coach outing, this year being a trip through North Wales to the seaside town of Rhyl. He was particularly excited since, though now aged eleven, he had never been to the sea, the nearest point being over 90 miles from his home. It was a grey day but the sun shone as the coach traversed the windy road through the Horseshoe Pass, an exquisite sight with the piles of rocks and views of the mountains. Unfortunately the skies became totally overcast, the sea was flat with very little wave motion, and both the beach and Rhyl seemed very unwelcoming.

Ken's siblings were all avid readers, particularly Keith who had several volumes about the histories of England and Egypt. Ken's main source of reading however continued to be comic books, and he was an avid reader, exchanging comics with a group of friends. Whilst horror comics started to gain much popularity, he preferred the Westerns and the stories about Kit Carson, Hopalong Cassidy and the Lone Ranger.

Keith was a major influence on both Ken and Roger through his love of knowledge. On many Saturdays Keith would take them on the train to Birmingham New Street Station with the aim of visiting both the main Museum and the separate Science Museum. On the first visit, Keith treated Ken and Roger to what became a regular feature, namely tea with beans on toast at a Café in Lewis's Department store. Ken decided he would like a little salt on his beans, picked up the cellar but then to his horror found he had poured sugar all over his meal. "Drat," he called out, much to Keith's amusement. The Natural History section of the Museum had a wide range of stuffed animals and birds and was a highlight for Ken, as was the Egyptian section (Keith's favourite) with its mummies and artefacts. After about three hours, Ken getting bored within one hour, the boys made their way to the Science Museum. Here there were some very interesting exhibits, with some interactive, such as challenging a machine to games such as noughts and crosses, and a transparent telephone switchboard. (Many years later, the Museum changed its location and incorporated at its entrance, the original London, Midland & Scottish (LMS) steam engine, the "City of Birmingham".)

With railway lines running at the rear of the house and along the upper level main line, it is little wonder that the boys developed an interest in "train spotting". The UK's railways were organized into regional branches such as the LMS and Great Western Railways (GWR). Each region had its own set of steam engines, together with "sheds", these being covered locations for housing and maintaining engines when not in use. The engines and sheds were all listed for each region in booklets, enabling train spotters to maintain records of engines that they had seen. The usual practice was to record the number and then to use a small ruler and pen to underline the number/name of an engine once spotted.

One curious feature of the LMS region was that trains from Euston to the north and to Scotland from London, would be routed either via Birmingham or they would bypass Birmingham completely, going via Lichfield, the two routes combining again from Stafford. This created an issue since the Lichfield route was often undertaken by the major expresses which were hauled by the fast and more powerful LMS "Coronation" and "Princess" Classes. The Coronation class included the set of so-called "semis", these being named after UK Cities, cities at that time being required to have a cathedral in order to attract such legal designation. No-one ever witnessed a Princess or City locomotive coming through the Dudley Port stations.

Two of Keith's friends, Derek and John, would tease Ken and Roger by saying that they had a secret location for spotting on the main line route through Lichfield. Eventually they agreed to take Ken and Roger one fine Sunday in summer, telling them they would need to use their bicycles. So off they went at 8:00 a.m. on a tortuous journey to Lichfield itself, some 20 miles away. On entering the City of Lichfield, the boys headed for Lichfield Trent Valley, where, on approaching a bridge in an open country area, they hauled their bikes over a fence and found themselves on a steep railway embankment looking down on a straight section of track. "Follow us and watch out for ant hills," said Derek, making his way along a narrow path at the top of the embankment. "This is a good spot," said John, laying his bike down and retrieving a blanket, bottle of pop and a sandwich, from his back-pack. The three others followed suit and within minutes a first train came by which to Ken's delight was the "Princess Elizabeth", a train spotting that was to stay in his memory throughout his life. The boys stayed for six hours spotting a range of LMS steam engines from the Princess, Coronation, Patriot, Royal Scot, Jubilee and Stanier classes. The journey back included the climb of an enormously long hill some six miles from Lichfield on the A461. "Stop," said Derek, "let's get bottles of pop from the shop at the foot of the hill." The pop was in a plain bottle, cost one penny and provided a wonderful taste on what had been a very warm and tiring day.

The following week the boys discovered that it was possible to get to Lichfield Trent Valley via a train to Birmingham New Street, a change to Lichfield City Station, and a bus from Lichfield City to Trent Valley. The return fare was quite cheap and a steady call on pocket money from paper rounds, but the trip proved a popular day out. Emboldened by such travel, Keith, Ken and Roger next ventured on cheap day returns to London, visiting such stations as Euston and St Pancras (both LMS), Paddington (GWR), and King's Cross (LNER, London North Eastern). Ken was especially thrilled on his first visit to King's Cross to spot the streamlined engine "Silver Link". On later trips to London, they visited Waterloo (Southern Railway), Liverpool Street station (LNER) and the enormously busy Clapham Junction. Ken had by this time got to know the Tube (London's underground) very well but had now visited London five times and had seen none of the tourist sites, only stations and the Tube!

The fascination with steam engines and train-spotting also led to visits to sheds including the holy grail of Crewe North. Locally, Bushbury, Wolverhampton, was a favourite, the boys accessing it via the canal and a perimeter fence. Such visits always created tension for the boys but Ken could not recall a single situation of being caught or chased off the premises by railway staff. The GWR shed at Oxley, Wolverhampton, was accessed via a steep grassy slope, but again was easy to enter and look around without being caught. This was not the case with Crewe, a major hub of the LMS. There were always hoards of train spotters there but it was nigh impossible to access the sheds, both the route to the sheds and the security staff being very big challenges. However one of the highlights of the boys' train spotting activities was the securing of a visitors pass to the Crewe railway works, such passes being akin to getting a Wimbledon ticket via their lottery system. What a thrill to see the wide range of steam engines, including an historic collection

24

featuring the original *Lion*. Ken was also fascinated by the assortment of bits and pieces hanging on walls above workbenches, including name plates of several engines.

Shortly before the summer break at the Grammar School, Ken learned that he had been chosen with a boy named Harry Jackson, to go on holiday to Weston-Super-Mare, Ken learning later that the holiday was sponsored by Tipton Rotary Club. Hilda packed a small suitcase for his first trip away from home and included underpants and pyjamas. Harry was catching a train at Tipton Owen Street and Ken at Dudley Port, the boys getting off at Birmingham New Street and heading to platform 10 for a connection to Weston-Super-Mare via Bristol Temple Meads. The Rotary Club had joint access to a hostel on the side of a hill at Weston, staff from the hostel waiting at the station and walking Harry and Ken to the rather grand stone building. The hostel included a large dining room, bathrooms and toilets and a large dormitory with single beds, hosting twelve boys from different parts of the country. Ken and Harry became friendly with two boys, Tom and George, from the town of Polesworth. The boys were subject to strict meal times, had to attend church on the Sunday, but were given freedom to explore and enjoy the beaches and the town during the daytimes. George still had the unfortunate habit of bed-wetting and was consequently taunted by the other boys in the dormitory. On the Wednesday afternoon, Tom, the only one with a watch, suddenly exclaimed "Hey, we are in trouble, it's after five and we are going to be late getting back for tea." George was a few yards away and Tom, Harry and Ken slyly and quietly agreed to push George into the paddling pool on the beach and claim that George had fallen in, making them late. This they did, George cursing them as they grabbed him and dropped him into the pool! But the ploy worked and the group were excused for being back late.

Bullying continued into Ken's second year at the Grammar School, the favourite trick being in the Latin class when three of the students surrounding him (Brian, Jimmy and Ron) would suddenly turn his desk upside down. Books would fall out as the top opened and ink would run over the floor. Ken, whose desk was alongside the classroom wall, would be accosted by the teacher and hit with a ruler. He wondered why the teacher, Mr Cartwright, did not appear to realize that it was not he that was messing about. However one day, after trying to hit Ken with a steel ruler, Mr Cartwright suddenly turned and whacked Ron across the head with the flat side of the ruler. This was the spur for Ken to decide he had had enough of bullying and he told the three boys, "You do that once more and I will hit you." Of course, they did not believe Ken who had always turned the other cheek. Over went the desk, up shot Ken and punched Brian. Clearly, Mr Cartwright did understand after all, looking the other way and ignoring the incident. Ken recalled later in life that no-one ever bullied him again at school. News had passed to the two boys from the next year who also stopped throwing stones at him. Sometimes one has to hit back and not turn the other cheek.

The incident at school also affected Ken's response to bullying outside of school, this only occurring from one boy on his paper round, a Roy James. As he entered Howard Street, there was Roy again, taunting and teasing him about being a "grammar grub" with holes in his shoes. Roy attempted a kick at Ken who promptly caught his foot, twisted his leg, put him on the floor, and knelt with his shins across Roy's arms. "Yo look here, if yo ever call me nerms again, I'll knock the livin dayloits out o ya." "Sorry," said Roy starting to cry. "I promise I wo do it again." Ken never had any more trouble from Roy. "Bullies can be real cowards," thought Ken, adding another element to his streetwise real life education.

It was during his second year that a major change occurred at Ken's Park Lane East home. Electricity was brought in and so the saga of broken gas mantles ceased. Ken stood at the entrance to the front room and flicked the light switch on and off, marvelling at the difference it made. Hilda shortly purchased a record player for the family. Bobby Darin's "Dream Lover" became a real favorite but was soon followed by the sounds of Elvis Presley, the Everly Brothers and the emergence of classical music and opera.

One weekend, trouble came to the family. Several of the boys Keith played with had taken to stealing apples and pears from Mr Copper's orchard, this being accessed by climbing over the garden wall, going down the railway bank, walking along the railway track in the direction of Great Bridge, climbing the bank beyond the road bridge, and then climbing the wall into the orchard. Mr Copper had become fed up with this and complained to the police who agreed to send Constable Kelly to keep his eye on things. There he was, waiting for the boys. Keith saw him and shouted to Trevor and Derek, who jumped back over the wall and started running along the track, Keith going the other way. Constable Kelly suspected the boys had started from Keith's garden and ran along the roadway to try to intercept them. At that time Ken was looking over the railway wall and saw Trevor and Derek running towards him. They climbed the bank and said "here Jamma, tek these, there's a copper ofter us." Ken was just about to take the fruit when he saw the copper charging up the garden. "I'll have you two little buggers," shouted PC Kelly, but he was too slow and off went Trevor and Derek towards the station, leaving the copper sprawling. He gave chase but the boys were too nimble and were never caught.

However Derek, Trevor and Keith were also guilty of stealing small bottles of orange juice from the dairy that lay at the top of the railway bank opposite Ken's back-garden, to the left of the Richards' home. They would hide the bottles under a strip of turf alongside the lower level railway bridge on Park Lane East. PC Kelly suspected the three boys and bided his time, catching them in the act just two weeks later. Fines and probation followed, all three being first offenders. The three were very lucky since it was common to commit older boys to a prison for youths, an approved school, known as "Borstal".

Then came an even bigger event. After being on the re-housing list for years, the family was allocated a council house on the nearby Denbigh Estate. Was this because the Council's required points count had been achieved, or because of the size and number of children, or was it because of the influence of Ken's Uncle Joe, who was a prominent local councillor? In any event it was amazing to move into a modern house with running water, a bathroom, indoor toilet, kitchen, and 3 bedrooms.

Chapter 3 Church and Social Life

Ken and his siblings were strongly encouraged to attend church and Sunday school, though their mother and father hardly ever attended. St Martin's was a Church of England school, the primary school being sandwiched between a historic graveyard and the church. One highlight was the Easter service, the children holding hands and encircling the church singing "Fight the good fight" and "There is a green hill far away" and then entering the church for the Easter service. The church had wonderful stained glass windows depicting several biblical scenes. The pinnacle of the church was in the shape of a pepper box, a local nickname for the building. The Vicarage was a very old rambling house, some 800 yards from the church in the parish of Dudley Port.

Ken always enjoyed the organ recitals and the hymn singing in the services, but was consistently bored by the vicar's sermon from the pulpit. He did gain some enjoyment from the banners giving the order of the service, checking for special features of the numbers such as primality and whether one number was the reverse of another. He was puzzled by the large number of religions in the world and why Christianity should be the "correct" religion, when others had a much greater number of followers. However he consoled himself with the following thoughts. Suppose Christianity was a myth, then believers and non-believers would be in the same boat at death. However if Christianity was not a myth then believers could secure eternal (infinite) life. So it must pay to be a believer!

Sunday school was again a chore and he sometimes skipped it with one or more of his siblings. Ken had a reasonable voice however, so much so that he would be asked from time to time to lead classroom singing from the front at school and was encouraged to join the church choir. Again he thoroughly enjoyed the singing but his acceptance of the strength of faith of his fellow choristers was destroyed one day when they passed around a girlie magazine during choir practice.

St Martin's held a party each year that everyone loved, namely the Garden Party hosted by the vicar, The Reverend Hamer, in the grounds of the Vicarage. This was a happy and colourful event with the community fully involved in the revelry and the games. The egg and spoon race saw children and parents participating, with tears flowing from some youngsters as the egg rolled off and smashed on the floor. The three-legged race was also a joy to watch, with a wide range of coordination skills demonstrated by the participants, the less skilled falling over onto the grass. Even more coordination was required in the sack race, with participants pitching forward as they lost their rhythm.

Directly opposite the Vicarage lay St Paul's Methodist Church, a very popular institution in the community. There were reasons for the popularity (a) the design of the church with the interior on two levels, the upper level fully encircling the church and with the organ and choir at the front of the upper level. This set-up seemed very conducive to full participation in hymn singing (b) the lower level of formality in the management structure of the Methodist church (c) the social facilities, including a stage in an adjoining room, permitting an extremely popular programme of amateur variety shows with comedy skits and accomplished vocal artists.

Ken had the good fortune to be given the opportunity to learn to play the violin during his first two years at the Grammar School but this was a great strain on the ears of his siblings and neighbours as he struggled to practice at home. Curiously, violin lessons clashed with a mathematics lesson each week but missing the mathematics class seemed to have no impact on his academic performance in the subject. Whilst he loved singing he had no natural feel for playing instruments and read the music and played the violin as if it were a mathematical exercise, thinking all the while where to place his fingers on the strings. He was one of a small group chosen to play at the morning assemblies in the Main Hall of the Grammar School and also featured once in playing at a practice session of a Midlands Schools Orchestra. However he had no doubt his siblings had sighed with relief when the violin teacher left the school and the instruments had to be returned to the storeroom, never to surface again! Music was however important to him and he revelled in the school choir, a feature of which was Christmas performances at a local church and at Retirement Homes.

Chapter 4 Adolescence

Ken was now entering his fourth year at the Grammar School and had to choose eight subjects, to be examined in the national Ordinary Level General Certificate of Education ("O" Level GCE), this covering England, Wales and Northern Ireland, but not apparently Scotland. The classes were divided into IV Arts, IV Science and IV General, the latter being for less academic students. Students in both the Arts and Science streams had to take core subjects such as Mathematics, a Science, English Language and either French or German. The IV Science students generally took Engineering Drawing, not surprising given the heavy industry in the Black Country and the plethora of openings in Drawing Offices, creating the blueprints for all sorts of engineering applications. However Ken had already demonstrated a failure to be other than scruffy and he had no artistic talent, unlike elder brother Keith. So he was denied entry to the class and was required instead to take History.

It was a curious feature of the History course that the greatest concentration was on the Royalist-Roundhead Civil War in England and on the French Revolution, the syllabus stopping prior to the Great War of 1914-1918. The highlight however was when Mr Greener, the teacher, asked the class "What happened to the earth dug up by those involved with the Gunpowder Plot?" As usual, the class dunce, Robert Walker, shot his hand up. "Yes, Walker," said Mr Greener. "Please Sir, they dug a hole and buried it," beamed Walker, absolutely sure of his answer. "Stupid boy," snapped Mr Greener, clipping Walker with a cane and cuffing his ears.

Ken's greatest issue lay with Chemistry, having never disclosed to anyone that he was colour blind, as was his mother and four of the five boys. Fortunately the class worked in pairs, his pal Jimmy Foster telling him the colour changes in experiments, Ken then carrying out the mathematical analysis. Physics was also an issue when it came to experiments concerned with the dispersion of light but somehow he survived the laboratory lottery, always drawing experiments where colour was not an issue.

It was the third week of term when Ken discovered he had been chosen for the first eleven football team, being selected at attacking left half-back, later to be named midfield. His *street cred* improved dramatically but he was never the best of players even though he was a regular goal scorer. Playing for the school created a logistic problem, since most games were on a Saturday morning, Ken then having to collect paper money later in the day and sometimes as he went delivering the evening papers. He was also grateful for the cover provided by his brother Roger. It was late in the Autumn when Ken suffered a painful foot injury. Dr Harrington diagnosed the problem as bruising but within a week he could no longer get his shoe on. A visit to the Dudley Guest Hospital's X-ray Department showed a multiple fracture, meaning that he was required to have a plaster cast and to use crutches. There was no school bus, the family did not of course own a car, and it was not feasible, given the bad weather, to walk the two miles on crutches, so he was required to stay at home, this lasting for 10 weeks.

Though he could not make school, he was still able to get around locally on crutches and visit his friend David Penn who lived in a small 2-up 2-down terraced home in Lower Church Lane. David's father, Jack, was registered blind and helped the family of four eke out a living by making cane baskets of all shapes and sizes, selling these on through the local Blind Institute. The main breadwinner was his wife Elizabeth, a beautiful lady, who always looked tired, spending her working life in a bedding factory. Though they had little themselves, they were the epitome of kindness to Ken. Jack, though a kind man who never complained about his loss of sight, ruled his two sons with a rod of iron, being ever mindful of the drudgery faced by Elizabeth. Ken was only too glad to help as much as he could, the week's chores including dusting and polishing the furniture and cleaning the windows. Jack would often say "if a job is worth doing it is worth doing properly," a philosophy that impacted on Ken with regard to his studies.

This philosophy, and Ken's apparent mathematical insight, had led to a problem in woodwork at school. Mr Woodruff had each member of the class design and manufacture a stool, instructing the class to plane the sections and use a ruler to check for flatness. "If you can see light coming through the edge of the ruler, then of course the section is not flat," said Mr Woodruff. Ken took this to heart, not thinking that one could never get exact flatness and one had to judge when one should stop. The outcome was a stool with three decent legs and one thin leg. "Stupid boy," said Mr Woodruff, clipping Ken across his head. The dovetailed joints were quite good and the stool was eventually glued up but never sat on!

Jack's philosophy also applied to cleaning bicycles, David and his brother Michael both possessing one. Once a month the bikes had to be stripped down, cleaned and oiled, so maintaining them in splendid working order. Both David and Michael had clear skills with mechanical objects; indeed Michael was serving his apprenticeship as a works mechanic, and was sponsored to take an Ordinary National Certificate in Engineering. He was some five years older than Ken, who stared with admiration as Michael completed his homework, handling complicated formulae in mathematics and physics and using a slide rule to carry out calculations. Ken never understood the operation of the slide rule and was of the generation that saw its use replaced by the electronic calculator.

His friendship with David also led to attendance at the Hebron Hall, a gospel hall run by a non-denominational group, allied to the Plymouth Brethren. He admired the fact that the group ran themselves without the formality or structures of the Church of England, the Roman Catholic Church, or even the Methodist Church. They allied themselves to the rallies of Billy Graham, Ken attending rallies in both Birmingham and Manchester. They also exchanged services with other such Halls and groups in the Midlands, members of the congregation, many in their teens, travelling in cars and a converted Bedford van. The group also carried out drives within the local population, going door to door to spread the Gospel and to seek recruits to their congregation. Sunday evenings were a favourite of Ken's, a subgroup meeting up at either a large house in an affluent suburb of Birmingham, owned by Mr

Evans, one of the elders of the Hall, or at a house on the Denbigh Estate. The activity consisted of singing gospel songs, and supping on tea, cake and sandwiches. Ken was always impressed by the sincerity of many of the faithful, including Mr and Mrs Evans and their children David, Rosemary and Jill. Ken had eyes for Jill, the youngest of the three children but she always appeared aloof and beyond his working class background. Rosemary did show interest in Ken, but he did not respond. David Penn was extremely strong physically, so arm wrestling with him was a complete no-no for anyone. He was also handsome and extremely popular with the girls, never being without a girlfriend and he eventually married Rosemary. This was unlike Ken, who notwithstanding having three sisters, remained extremely shy.

One of the pressures exerted by elders, and at the Billy Graham rallies, was to declare one's faith and to be "saved", though this was not obligatory. Being saved also led to baptism by submersion, the Hebron Hall containing a structure for carrying out this event. Ken felt he believed in God but was never sufficiently convinced of the notion of being "saved". Since early childhood he had always asked himself the question "who made God? Or who or what preceded God?" It was later that he realized that people were always seeking an answer to the question of eternal life, that is looking to plus infinity in time. Why not consider minus infinity in time and accept that God had always existed, thus answering the fundamental question? It also answered the question of "the Big Bang". If God and materials had always existed then it seemed that at some stage certain materials came together in the universe, galaxies were formed and the ongoing coming together of materials created further galaxies. Somewhat of a worry was that a mathematical approach also included the concept of open and closed intervals. Thus, perhaps the end of life coincided with a closed interval, life ceasing completely at that point. On the other hand, a quick glance at the heavens suggested that there was a greater being, and that "my Father's house has many mansions" was a reference to infinity, there being a place for an infinite number of people and creatures in heaven. Ken marvelled at the skies and the stars. Is there a simple solution to the universe in that it is infinite in every direction? At the same time he marvelled at the microscope and how it suggested the concept of infinitely small. So are the scientists never to be satisfied as they moved from atoms to subatomic particles and ever decreasing magnitudes of structures?

Besides local and regional activities, the Gospel Hall interacted at national level, including organizing seaside holidays at a Christian hostel in Llanfairfechan in North Wales. Ken was able to join a group who travelled in the Bedford van and spent a week there, mixing in fellowship with similar groups from Gospel Halls and churches around the U.K. One of the highlights was a walk to the top of Mount Snowdon, the second highest peak (at 1085 meters) in the U.K. The group ascended the mountain, following the Snowdon railway line. As they approached the top, the mist descended and was extremely dense, making observation of the line difficult and with the danger of losing one's way. Eventually however, the summit was reached and a hot drink at the café there was more than welcome. With great fortune, or divine intervention, the clouds and mist cleared, giving spectacular views of the knife edge ridge below and of Lake Padarn. "Time to descend," said the group's guide and off they went down the so-called Pig Track, being met at the bottom by a coach that took the party back to the hostel.

Returning to school after the mending of his broken foot and after the Christmas holiday, Ken realized that he had missed a lot of stuff and resolved to buckle down and study whilst keeping his sporting activity going and getting his paper round back. "Back with us, are you Jukes?" said the form teacher Mr Marsh. "Enjoy your holiday?" he continued in his usual sarcastic manner as he checked the register. "Yes Sir," replied Ken, thinking "here we go again." However his attitude to study had changed and he started to enjoy the classes, soon catching up by reading in the evenings and weekends. Lo and behold, at the end of the Spring term he moved from his regular 14th position in the class of 28 to 3rd overall. This acted as a tremendous spur, so much so that he came top of the class in the end of year exams.

The summer flew by as did Year 5, at the end of which Ken had to take his national Ordinary Level exams in eight subjects. The mock exams went well and were soon followed in June by the real thing, exams taking place in Willingsworth, a new secondary modern school, with independent invigilators (proctors). Ken was determined to seek employment in the summer and was fortunate to be able to secure a position of Wages Clerk at the nearby Midlands Electricity Board (the MEB). The MEB was housed in an imposing modern multi-storey building with canteen facilities and extensive sports grounds. Training was given but the work was very straightforward, each Clerk having a large work-board and a book of income tax tables. Starting from individual time sheets, a hand written spreadsheet was set up for each employee, the work requiring simple arithmetic and the taking into account of special rates such as overtime and "dirty money". An Office Manager and his Deputy sat at the front of some 15 Wages Clerks, all male, and were called upon on occasions to answer queries. However their main activities seemed to be working through huge sheets of computer output, this being generated from the work of some 60 comptometer operators, all female, who were all working in an adjoining room on data input. The company providing the machinery and producing the overall output was International Business Machines, IBM!

Ken was curious as to a system that could produce so much paper and he wondered what the output was all about. The Deputy Manager was struggling with some output from a program and asked Ken if he had any ideas. This was his second exposure to computer programming, the first having been on the valve machine, the *Witch*, in the basement of Wolverhampton Technical College, where he had been given the opportunity to code a "sums" program in machine code and to run it on paper tape through the machine. Ken studied 10 of the pages of output at the MEB and soon noticed an inconsistency with similar cases that should have given identical results. A check on the code soon led to identification of the error in the program. The Deputy Manager brought Ken's observations to the attention of the Manager and subsequently to IBM, whose rep asked Ken if he would like to join the company. "Thanks, but no," said Ken, his objective being to stay on at school and enter the lower sixth form.

It was early August when he was given leave from the MEB to report to the Grammar School to collect his results. He was relieved to be told by the Headmaster that he had passed all eight O-levels and with high marks, including a score of 85% in Physics and 75% in both Mathematics and Chemistry, the highest in the School. Next came choice of the three subjects to be studies at Advanced-Level, this being a real dilemma due to his colour blindness, the national exam in Chemistry including an individual practical. After much discussion, he decided to take Physics and two Mathematics subjects. No-one had ever before taken both A-level Mathematics and A-level Further Mathematics at the school, Ken finding later that he and a second student, Paul Turner, had opted for this combination and so they would be in a class of two for Further Mathematics.

He thoroughly enjoyed his final two years at school, the experience being made more enjoyable through being chosen to captain the school at cricket and football in the upper sixth form. Further, by running around his paper rounds twice a day for six days each week, he continued to do well in the cross-country and mile races. His greatest challenge came from Jimmy, now a member of the famous Tipton Harriers Club, Jimmy and Ken exchanging wins from time to time. Both of them also played chess for the school and for their schoolmasters' team in the Kipping League, their rivalry crossing many frontiers.

Christmas in the Lower Sixth saw a change in direction for Ken. He and others had been invited to a New Year's party at a house owned by a girl named Pauline in the Fourth year. Jimmy and Ken ended up going out with Pauline and her friend Carol, respectively, the start of a long relationship for Ken. This also led to the end of his close friendship with David Penn and cessation of activity with the Gospel Hall.

The summer soon arrived, Ken working again at the Midlands Electricity Board as a Wages Clerk. The work was extraordinarily routine, with nothing having changed with regard to data input, use of IBM machines and the manual work with time sheets and the determination of weekly wages.

Life in the Upper Sixth was dominated by the oncoming national A-level exams and application for University and College entrance. Many of the girls were interested in teaching careers, which were mainly achieved through two-year training colleges. "Jukes," said Form Master Mr Rogers in a one to one conversation, "if you want a life with holidays and little money, then teaching is a good profession, otherwise choose another direction." "Yes Sir," this advice making Ken think about careers. "I would like to go to university and have a career in electronics, Sir." "Good luck with your applications Jukes; that seems to be an emerging area and I foresee the end of the heavy industry that forms the basis of the job market here in the Black Country."

It was rare for anyone from the School to apply to Oxford or Cambridge. There were two reasons: the Headmaster, himself an MA Cantab, did not encourage pupils in that direction, particularly boys whose accent was broad Black Country and who he felt would not fit in socially at Oxbridge. Secondly, Oxbridge had their own entrance exams and in order to stand a realistic chance, one would need to spend a further year at school and take Special A-Levels, a path which for most families was beyond their financial means.

There was no limit on the number of applications one could make to universities, Ken's selection including courses in electronics, physics and engineering at Sheffield and Durham. His first interview was at Sheffield University, Ken taking a train to Birmingham New Street and changing there for Sheffield. It was a very foggy day and the fog never lifted all day. The interview went well and included questions on the nature of atomic power stations and the work of Einstein. Ken struggled with his answers but was helped by the posters at Tipton Grammar on Calder Hall and visits arranged by the school to the Electricity Board Centre at Worcester and to Stourport Power station. He was subsequently offered a place provided he achieved the minimum qualifications of two "40%" scores at A-Level, i.e. two bare passes. The train journey home was tortuous with the fog having become extremely dense by the time he reached Birmingham, the station announcer then informing passengers that all trains to Tipton had been cancelled. "Bugger me," he thought on also learning that all buses had ceased to run. Telephones were not yet part of normal family life and so he decided there was nothing he could do but walk the ten miles home. He had reached Swan Village, one of his favourite places to train spot GWR engines, when out of the fog appeared four number 74 buses crawling along in the fog in the direction of West Bromwich. These were the only buses he saw in the 10 mile walk, the end of which came as a great relief. "Hello Ken," said Hilda as he entered the kitchen, "and how did the trip go?" She was shocked to hear his account of the day and how he had walked home from Birmingham New Street station. "Go and sit down whilst I pour you a hot cup of tea." He wandered into the lounge where Keith, Roger, Norma, David and Dawn were sitting watching TV and baking in the heat of a roaring fire. No-one was interested in what Ken had been through since this was outside the experience of everyone, no-one in the family or their relatives having been to university,

The summer approached and A-level exams took place in a local church hall. On completion, the upper sixth form were not required to attend school except for the last day of the term. In the meantime Ken accepted provisional offers from Sheffield and Durham, the latter to major in Physics. He again looked to secure a summer job but the Electricity Board was no longer offering any positions and it was extremely difficult to secure an opening anywhere. Eventually, through Uncle Joe's influence, he was offered a place at Walsall Conduits, working on a production line making light fittings for petrol pumps. The pay was extremely poor, Ken being on a fixed wage whereas all other members of the line were on piecework, their wages depending on how many light fittings were produced in the 5 day week. His role in the production line was to receive an aluminium box and to drill 16 holes using a drill mounted in a stand. The edges of the box were quite rough and required him to wear thick gloves which protected against the waste aluminium and also from touching the hot drill bit. The work became extremely mind numbing and was made worse by the fact that he had to keep up with the production of drilled boxes.

The last week of July and first week of August formed the traditional industrial holiday weeks in the Midlands. Ken was kept on by Walsall Conduits but, with the production line at a standstill, his role was as an industrial painter, cleaning up and then painting the myriad of machines in the huge factory floor. He wondered what the reaction would be as the men and women returned to machines cleaned and painted in awful colours by a colour blind painter!

And so the day of publication of A-level results arrived, students having to queue outside the Headmaster's Office and be told verbally of their results. Ken did quite well having the highest scores in the Sciences, and qualifying for both Sheffield and Durham. The latter would apparently involve studying at King's College and using facilities at Durham Castle. But he had a dilemma since both Electronic Engineering and Physics involved certain work which he felt would be impacted by his colour blindness. He discussed this with his Mathematics teacher Mr Hinchliffe, a brilliant teacher with exceptional skills in managing discipline in his classes, and who got 100% of his O-level class to achieve a pass. Mr Hinchliffe had taken him to Wolverhampton Technical College to meetings of a mathematics club, this opening up the world of mathematics to Ken, the club also showing animated mathematics films.

"Jukes," said Mr Hinchliffe, "how about studying mathematics instead? There is an interesting situation at the University College of Wales, Aberystwyth, where a new campus has been opened and a new group of academics from Cambridge and London universities have been recruited in statistics and mathematics." A letter was written to the Registrar and to Ken's disappointment no place was offered. This was queried and it was discovered that an administrative error had been made, an unconditional offer of a place then being made to him by the University College of Wales.

Chapter 5 University Student Life

Hilda was very proud of her son having achieved a University place but was very worried about the financial implications. The good thing was that Ken had secured a full grant covering tuition fees, accommodation and meals in a Hall of Residence, and a small allowance for books and general living. Although he was the first in the family to go to university, Hilda had some knowledge of what that entailed. Some 3 years earlier, her close friend Mrs Caesar had allowed her daughter Winny to stay an extra year in the sixth form so as to take the S-level exams and apply for entrance to Oxford University. Winny had secured a place to read History, much to Hilda's and Mrs Caesar's delight.

What particularly worried Hilda was the lack of money to support Ken who had just £20 from his summer job at Walsall Conduits and what would happen if his grant from the local authority did not come through in time? She was aware that he would need to pay the annual Hall of Residence fee and to purchase books and an undergraduate gown. And then, just one day before he was due to leave for university, tragedy struck the family, Hilda becoming ill and an ambulance being called by Auntie Dot.

Ken left for university the next day, taking the high level train to Wolverhampton and switching to Wolverhampton low level where he boarded the "Cambrian Express" for a first visit to Aberystwyth. On arrival there he carried his case to the front of the station and asked a porter how to get to Pantycelyn Hall on Penglais Hill. "Take the bus here," said the porter pointing to a double decker at the front of the station. He was one of several boys on the bus, discovering later that no Halls of Residence were mixed. The bus struggled up a long hill before stopping across the road from Pantycelyn. Off the passengers struggled, all with cases, and entered the imposing and stylish building overlooking the town and sea. The boys were met in the hallway by the bursar, a lady in her 50's and were given keys to their assigned rooms. Ken had been allocated a double room on the second floor, in the far corner of the building. It had the advantage of windows at the side and front and with a view of the sea in the distance. The room contained two single beds, two desks with chairs and reading lamps, two small bookshelves and a washbasin and rail, the latter being hidden by a folding door. The beds were covered with beautifully patterned heavy Welsh blankets. Half way down the corridor were bath and shower facilities. Immediately outside the room was a tiny facility called a gyp room, equipped with hot plates, a kettle and a toaster. Ken was thrilled with the wonderful facilities but was apprehensive about who would be his room-mate. He also discovered that his room was cleaned and his bed made daily, apart from Sundays. Was this the way the other half lived?

There was a knock on the door and in came Ron Aspinall, Ken's room-mate for the year. "Hello," said Ron, introducing himself, the two boys quickly agreeing on beds and desks. Ron was also in his first year and was majoring in Geography. He hailed from Tettenhall, Wolverhampton, having been Head Boy at a new Comprehensive School there. He was a keen and accomplished Rugby Union player and had a quiet, friendly demeanour. Ron had arrived by car with his mother and father and left the room to say his goodbyes.

Ken now wandered around the building, which had a large student Common Room, a huge Dining Room accommodating all 180 student residents, a Senior Common Room where the wardens hosted small parties for dinner, a Nursing Bay, a television lounge, a small unmanned library, and a laundry room with washing machines and driers. This was all a far cry from Ken's upbringing and it would be some time before he adjusted to the new situation. A bell rang signalling dinner, as explained on the fact sheet about the Hall. He made his way down and joined a long queue that snaked through the kitchen collecting meals on trays. There were six long lines of dining tables the length of the dining room, each table hosting about 10 boys, with seating on benches. Gaps between tables allowed access to each side of the tables. At the opposite end to the kitchen was a platform, with a dining table for the Warden, his guests, if any, and two Sub-wardens. There was no seating plan for the boys, the freshers being noticeable by their quietness and the juniors and seniors congregating together and totally ignoring the freshers. Following a welcome and introduction by the Warden, himself a Historian from Cambridge University, the students moved to the Common Room, again dominated by the returning students, many with Welsh accents but many also with cultured English accents. The Common Room had a wide collection of newspapers and magazines, Ken hiding away behind these but actually listening to the many conversations around him. Ron and Ken settled easily into sharing a room, and soon teamed up somewhat with neighbours Iestyn and Robert, the latter having attended public school in Bristol. Ken was the only one doing mathematics and a football player and had little in common with Iestyn or Robert.

The first week was an orientation period involving registration, confirmation of classes with an academic adviser, and signing up for student organizations and various sports trials. Ken's adviser suggested that he study Physics but he turned this down, agreeing instead on Pure Mathematics, Applied Mathematics and Statistics. He was very relieved to find that his grant for the Autumn term had arrived and with the Hall fees having been met, he was aware that the residue needed to be paid into a bank. He opened an account in the Trustees Savings Bank, his first bank account!

Orientation events took place in the original college buildings located on the sea front. The promenade also included the main girls' Hall of Residence, Alexandra Hall, and various smaller Halls for boys. Ken's classes however were to be held in a magnificent new building just a short walk from Pantycelyn. The new building had a splendid curved front, was some seven storeys high, and gave outstanding views of the town and sea. The first floor, dedicated to Physics, included a large lecture theatre strutting out of the front of the building and clad in stone. The upper floor comprised the library for pure and applied mathematics, physics and statistics.

Ken maintained contact with Carol, writing and receiving letters almost every day. However some two weeks after starting university, Dr Price, a sub-warden, knocked Ken's door around 7:00

p.m. and said that he had received a phone call saying that Hilda was extremely ill and unlikely to survive the night. Ron stepped in with characteristic kindness, agreeing that Dr Price drive Ken to Shrewsbury train station and arranging for Ron's father to meet Ken at Wolverhampton station and take him home to Tipton.

It transpired that Hilda was in quarantine at Moxley hospital and had been diagnosed with the most serious form of meningitis. Reg told him about the situation and advised him not to try to visit that night but to remember Hilda as she had been. It was in the early hours that Hilda tragically passed away at the age of just 50.

Ken returned to university after much discussion and reflection. Should he carry on at university? How would the family survive? Margaret had married Tony that Easter and so the burden had fallen on Norma, then aged just 15 and who bravely acted as a surrogate mother. Clive himself had also left the family home some years before, first sharing a room with Ted at the grandparents' home, then going to live with Ted and Dot after their marriage and then securing his own flat. Ken decided that he had to justify being at university and to try and make a success of his time there. One quick decision was to withdraw from playing chess or cricket and to limit himself to study and to football, playing in the local league for Pantycelyn.

The classes in Statistics were given by the eminent Statistician Prof D.V. Lindley, a brilliant lecturer and an international devotee of Bayesian theory. He was joined by a team of statisticians, several later becoming Professors around U.K. universities, including Stone, Bartholomew and King. During one introductory class on probability, Prof Lindley did a survey of the students asking each how many brothers and sisters they had. When it came to Ken he answered 7, only to be queried whether he was answering honestly. Did Prof Lindley not believe in outliers in data!

The term passed slowly, Ken's favourite subject being Real Analysis in Pure Mathematics, the lecturer being John Clegg, a Cambridge graduate, who was also a famous concert pianist, and who featured on BBC radio. Besides excellent formal lectures, Mr

Clegg ran small tutorial groups of 4 to 5 students in his office, clarifying difficulties in the subject and with the added pleasure of handing around a box of Clarnico Creams! A particular thrill was an invitation to his home where he and his wife entertained a small group of students with appetisers followed by dinner and a short recital on the grand piano in the large lounge.

Ken became engaged to Carol that Christmas, Carol actually buying the ring, Ken having just two shillings and sixpence left from his term's maintenance grant. On returning to College in January, he was pleased to see on the Notice Board that he had passed the mid-term exams in Pure Mathematics, Applied Mathematics and Statistics, all with First Class Grades. He was adjusting to College life and to the enormous gulfs in "class" and backgrounds of the students. Indeed, on the Cambrian Express journey back to College, he shared a compartment with two fellow students from Harrow, who enquired, seemingly through their noses, "Do they have sales in the Provinces?"

The academic year passed slowly and finished with end of year examinations. Results were posted on the Board in the Mathematics building, Ken being pleased to learn that he had again been classified as First Class in both Pure Mathematics and Statistics but there were no classifications given in Applied Mathematics, just pass or fail. This caused a problem since he had to choose two of the three subjects to take in his second year. Pure Mathematics was the subject he loved most and given he did not know the detailed result in Applied Mathematics, he chose to study Statistics also.

Following his return from University, Ken was invited to visit the Grammar School to talk about his university experience and what university mathematics was like. As was the normal protocol, he first called in on the Headmaster. "Come in," said the Head as Ken knocked on his door. "Ahh Brown, good to see you here. How is Nottingham University treating you and are you coping well with Chemistry?" Ken corrected the Head, thinking to himself, how could he not know me, the captain of the school football and cricket teams, the prize-winner for best A-level performance in Science &

Mathematics and the first to do mathematics at university. "Ahh, of course," said the Head without conviction and excusing himself.

Ken was once again faced with little money in the summer, managing at the last minute to secure a position of porter at Oldbury Railway Goods Yard, alongside Glass's factory and the main London-Birmingham-Wolverhampton LMS line. Training was given on driving 3-wheeler Scammel vehicles, these being hooked up to long trailers that mainly transported glass or steel coils. They were also used for shipping the contents of numerous railway wagons, the emptying and sweeping of which constituted the main bulk of Ken's working day. He found it quite difficult to handle the clutch of the Scammel and to reverse the trailers, these swinging quickly into the side of the cab.

It transpired that Horace, the weighbridge attendant at the yard, was to be away for two weeks. "Horace," said Joe the Foreman, "there's a young kid emptying wagons who does sums at university. Can yo gie him a half day helping out with the weighbridge, tache him the ropes, and let us know if he con handle it while yo'm away." So Ken was called from the yard to work with Horace. "Now look here lad," said Horace," the only thing to watch out for from these buggers is chayting about the weight of the steel coils. They will try and put only two or three wheels on the weighbridge platform and then call at a scrap yard and pocket the money they get for the extra coils!" Sure enough, Monday came, and the second driver, who was delivering steel coils, had just three wheels fully on the weighbridge. Ken jumped up quickly, opened the window and shouted "Ay yow! GET ALL THEM FUCKING WHEELS ON THERE OR I'LL HAVE YO!" The message was quickly received that he was no pushover and no further incidents occurred. Ever since working at Walsall Conduits, he had realized that working men and factory workers used Chaucerian language as a matter of course, even though, like Tony, they would never use such language at home or in front of women. Though he could swear with the best, Ken had come back from College with a reduction in the severity of his Black Country accent, especially elongating bath (baarth) and garage

46

(garaage), but it had taken him only a couple of weeks to get back into the local accent.

Ken spent much time with Carol over the summer, her parents being extremely generous, treating him as a son, notwithstanding the demands of having six children themselves. They had a car and dropped Ken at Pantycelyn for his second year of study. He had been allocated a single room over the main entrance, room 13, it being rumoured that students allocated to that room generally failed the year! Rooms continued to be cleaned daily and beds made by the cleaners! Ken was also particularly fortunate to have a wonderfully gracious lady, quite advanced in years, who treated him in a very motherly fashion, even to the extent of washing and drying any clothes and towels he had left around the room. It was a life of luxury really but tempered with the need for self-discipline in studying.

As in his first year, the Hall management maintained the policy of bed linen to be changed weekly, the system including sending these to an outside laundry. All meals continued to be supplied within the Hall fees, with Sunday lunch being formal, everyone being required to wear an academic gown. Following Sunday lunch, it was traditional to continue to wear your gown and walk outside the front of Hall along a short stretch of lane leading to the imposing building of the National Library of Wales. The flower beds in front of the Library were splendid as were the views over the town, over Cardigan Bay, and to the south. One could also see the Devil's Bridge narrow gauge railway, a big tourist attraction in Aberystwyth.

The second year passed slowly with one highlight being a soccer match for Pantycelyn against a student team at Cardiff University. A coach took the team through the Plynlimon mountain range in mid-Wales and went to Cardiff via the pretty towns of Rhayader and Llandrindod Wells, the latter having many black and white buildings. Ken at the time was playing as an inside forward and had one of those days when everything goes right, scoring all 5 goals in a 5-0 win. Another success was the achievement of First Class passes in both Pure Mathematics and Statistics in the end of year exams.

His summer was dominated by working for the same company as his father, Stordy Engineering of Wolverhampton. This was the first time he had any real contact with or help from his father. Reg was continually working away from home, had no bank account and sent money back to Norma by registered mail. As had been the case when Hilda was alive, Reg however did not have a regular method of or commitment to sending money from his wages, so there were times when Norma had no income to sustain those at home. Ken found out later that Clive was bailing Reg out as best he could when money failed to arrive.

Ken's designation with Stordy's was as a steel erector, the role helping support the installation of significant heat treatment plant at firms throughout the U.K., Reg also working abroad on a number of occasions. The firm operated through a lead engineer on the staff of the company, who would recruit local labour from the town where they would be carrying out a job. Ken's first assignment was at Coventry Radiators, working with Stordy Engineer Sam Thompson, installing a large heat treatment plant. His work usually involved assembly routines, similar he thought to working with a giant Meccano/Erector set, but also involving at times the use of industrial drills to create the holes for large bolts in the metal structure of the plant. The engineer directed the work, being skilled in reading off from large blueprints. This particular plant was some 12 feet high and Ken was frequently working on the top, climbing there on a steel ladder built into the design of the plant. Sam asked Scott, a muscular fellow, one of the steel erectors, to pass Ken a large industrial drill having a steel cross piece in the handle some 2 feet wide, allowing one's weight to be put behind the drill. Scott held the drill in one hand and put the other hand onto the steel ladder. There was a flash and a bang and he was immediately thrown back onto the floor but was able to let go of the drill. It transpired that the drill had no plug on the end, the bare wires having been pushed into an industrial extension lead that was already in use and had shorted out as soon as Scott touched the metal ladder. It was fortunate that Scott had not been killed and that no Safety Officer was around since it would quite likely have spelled serious trouble for Stordy Engineering.

Ken's second job was at a plant in Banbury and involved both fun and danger. This time Reg was the Engineer and he and Ken stayed at an old coaching inn, sharing a room with two single beds, the sheets of Reg's having a couple of holes. "Let's go down and eat," said Reg who asked the hotel proprietor where the dining room was. "Did you know King Charles II stayed here once?" said the proprietor to Reg who immediately replied with typical Black Country deadpan humour "Did he? Tell him to take off his spurs next time before he gets into bed." The job was a two day affair, requiring the completion of a large heating oven, some 12 feet high, connection to an electricity supply and then testing. A casual steel erector, Fred, was working with Ken and asked him to get inside the lower section of the oven and to be ready for a large U-tube which Ken was to bolt inside. Fred passed the U-tube into the oven through the two 6 inch diameter holes in the casing but the fit was a little tight. Fred climbed onto an electricity supply box and gave the U-tube an enormous whack with a large hammer. The sensation for Ken was like standing next to bells in a church belfry, his ears ringing and giving him a sensation of deafness. "You fucking idiot," he shouted to Fred as he clambered out of the oven.

The next job was a very substantial one at Reed's factory in Liverpool, working with Stordy Engineer Arthur Manning, who had recruited Jeff, another casual steel erector locally. "Ken, first go and get yourself lodging nearby," said Arthur. So off he went and headed for adverts on the window of a nearby newspaper shop. Sure enough lodgings were advertised and he went and found the location. He was absolutely horrified to be offered an unfurnished room in a dreadful hovel, a run-down property with a broken bed, no other furniture, no bathroom and an outside toilet. "No thanks," said Ken to the owner, the property reminding him of Fagan's rooms in Charles Dickens' Oliver Twist. The second advert turned out to be from a small casino with comfortable rooms and at a very reasonable rent and he jumped at it.

He reported back to Arthur, who explained what the job entailed, using a set of blueprints to illustrate his explanation. Reed's factory painted beer and soft drink cans for a huge variety of customers. The drying systems involved the cans resting on a moving wire with the cans passing through a set of connected small ovens running for about 80 yards, the line to be replaced being some 30 feet in the air with a narrow steel walkway running alongside. Work started each day at 8:00 a.m. and was scheduled as a 12 hour day. The new system was to be constructed alongside the old existing system but on the opposite side of the walkway. So Ken started working on the installation, him and the other erector soon realizing that the heat from the existing oven was to make them sweat profusely. Further, the noise levels in the factory were extreme as the cans raced around the various lines. Arthur halted the trio at 12:00 noon and off they went to a local pub for an hour, where they each downed three pints of shandy (a beer and lemonade mixture), replacing the body liquid lost from sweating. This was accompanied with a huge cheese and onion sandwich, the bread slices being 1 inch thick and cut by the landlord's wife from beautifully fresh loaves! Time passed quite quickly given the size of the job and at 6:00 p.m. Arthur called the two steel erectors to his bench. "I need to fill your time sheets in each day. Right, sign here for today, 8:00 a.m. to 8:00 p.m. you bloody liars," said Arthur winking at Ken and Jeff. And that day was repeated over the next two weeks. It was now time for testing and so Arthur set up a trial, turning the new ovens on and, when heated, passing a string of cans along, only for the system to immediately jam up! "Oh, fuck it, what a bastard system," exclaimed Arthur returning to check the blueprint drawings. Ken looked over the drawings with Arthur and very soon noticed that the gap between the walls of the ovens had not taken into account the coefficient of expansion. "Well bugger me," said Arthur "you are right. Let's recalibrate the width." So next day the team started adjusting the sides of the ovens parallel to the transport wire, taking another week to complete and test the new system. It would not be the last time that Ken observed problems in industry, reminding him, as with his own wooden stool, that one needed to be practical rather than exact.

And so the summer passed by and it was time to return to College, Ken having chosen to major in Pure Mathematics, taking six subjects in his Honours Year, namely Complex Variable, the Calculus of Variations, Group Theory, Projective Geometry, Differential Geometry and The Theory of Numbers. It was curious that of the 26 students in the Honours Year, just two had decided to opt to major in Applied Mathematics, both students being Welsh and being First Class candidates. Each subject in Pure Mathematics was demanding and Ken soon got his head down. He had been allocated a small single room facing the sea in Pantycelyn but soon found music from other rooms and a somewhat claustrophobic atmosphere were not conducive to deep thinking. He tried out the National Library but was put off there by the constant noise of students and librarians walking around the library. He eventually settled on working in the small library at the front of Pantycelyn, normally only himself and a classmate, Dai Prosser, using the facility. By this time and with constant study, Dai and Ken had each developed a form of photographic memory. This became apparent as they queued for meals. Working on Complex Variable, for example, Ken would quote a theorem number in his notes and Dai would quote the theorem before testing Ken in a similar manner.

April came around and Ken had the same birthday as Robert, a neighbour in his fresher year. As was the custom, Ken and Robert invited friends to a birthday celebration to be held at the White Lion Pub at Talybont, some 8 miles north of Aberystwyth, the village having two pubs next door to each other, one called the White Lion, the other the Black Lion. Again as customary, Ken and Robert sat at opposite ends of a long table and were challenged at regular intervals to down a pint in one go. Needless to say they were both legless at the end of the dinner. The group of 12 piled into three cars and were driven to the beach at nearby Borth where Ken and Robert were carried to and dumped into the sea, both wearing their best suits. It was damn cold being late April and the two boys soon came to their senses and were pulled out before being driven to Pantycelyn and dumped on the beds in their rooms. Robert suffered a second indignity when boys in a neighbouring room took off the door to his room and hid it on the roof of Pantycelyn.

Final exams, three hours in each subject, took place in early June, Ken being alarmed to find that his six exams took place in the morning and afternoon of Monday and Tuesday, Wednesday morning and Thursday morning. The exam period ran over three weeks but he would be finished in the first four days and would have virtually no time to revise between exams. By the end of the fifth exam on Wednesday morning he was utterly exhausted mentally and decided to try and blow his mind clear with a game of golf. This did the trick and he prepared that evening for his sixth and final exam, the subject being Differential Geometry. None of Ken's friends had anything like his exam schedule and so on the Thursday lunchtime he packed his case and caught the train back to the Midlands. The results were to be published some six weeks later and so Ken hitch-hiked to Aberystwyth, after first taking a bus to Tettenhall on the north side of Wolverhampton. Besides lifts from Carol's father, Ken had hitch-hiked on a number of occasions, it being very common for cars and trucks to pick up people, particularly once you reached the Welshpool/ Gobowen fork in the A5 on the north-west side of Shrewsbury. The usual hitch – hike journey time was four to five hours. Starting out at 8:00 a.m., Ken arrived at the College at 1:00 p.m. and made his way to the Mathematics building only to find the building locked. Peering through the glass doors he could see that the results had been posted on the far board but was unable to read them, the building not re-opening until 2:00 p.m! He made his way down the hill for lunch at the Cooper's pub and then returned with some trepidation. However he was elated to see that two students had been awarded First Class Honours, Ken and his study friend Dai Prosser.

Ken was asked to meet with the Head of Department, Prof W. B. Pennington, a brilliant teacher and also the Editor of one of the UK's premier Mathematics Research Journals, the Journal of the London Mathematical Society. Ken had indicated that he would like to pursue a PhD and he was informed that he would qualify for a postgraduate studentship from the Science Research Council. However two weeks later, Prof Pennington wrote to him saying that he had been nominated for and awarded the Dr Samuel Williams Scholarship of the University of Wales, this being more prestigious, having been won in competition with nominees from other subjects.

One of his footballing friends, John Roberts, was also returning to College to pursue Teacher Training, the two agreeing to meet up in Aberystwyth to find lodgings, Halls of Residence not permitting postgraduate students to stay in them. They discovered that the Castle Hotel, just off South Beach, was offering 12 places for the first time and the two boys met up with the owners Major and Mrs Clark, and secured a shared double bedroom, with breakfasts and Sunday lunch also being included.

It was again crucial to get a summer job, Ken being pleased that Reg had again been able to arrange for him a position with Stordy Engineering as a steel erector. His first assignment was working with another Stordy Engineer, Dick Graham. The task was at Wythenshaw, Manchester, a relatively simple one requiring the movement of a large control box on the factory floor of an international electrical company. The box was disconnected from the power supplies and the four bolts holding it to the concrete floor removed. Additional men were called to help load the box onto a very low trailer and move it to its new location. Once there, the position of the four new holes for the bolts were marked on the concrete floor and Ken had the task of using a pneumatic drill, known as a kango hammer, to drill them. The noise and vibration of the kango hammer made for an uncomfortable task but the overall job had been completed by mid-day on the second day. Off went Dick to see one of the works managers to get the job signed off, only to find that the plant engineers had changed their relocation plans, the control box having to be disconnected and moved to a third location!

The next day, Ken caught a train to Ellesmere Port on the Wirral in Cheshire where he reported to Reg and Joe Duncan, a second supporting Stordy Engineer. Reg informed Ken that lodgings had been arranged with him and so he immediately started work on installation of a sequence of very large ovens and a moving track for passing painted manufactured items through the ovens. At about 6:00 p.m. the team stopped and made their way to the lodgings where, following an evening meal, the landlady, a rather large lady in her late fifties, Joe, Ken and Reg squeezed into a taxi which took them to a local working men's club. The club had a stage and bar and four rows of tables, these extending from close to the stage right back to the far wall. The room was absolutely packed and the beer flowed profusely whilst at the same time a series of singers performed from the stage bringing the audience into the old songs. The group, all the worse for wear, crammed into a taxi for the return journey, Ken immediately making for the shared bedroom and deciding he would give such evenings a miss in the future. Saturday came along, still a full working day, and Ken, after work and wearing dark grey flannels and a black blazer with the University badge displayed prominently, decided to take a bus into Chester, a nearby historic Roman town. After exploring the town and Dixie Dean's bar, he found himself outside Quaintways, a club with dining on the ground floor, ballroom dancing on the middle floor and rock and roll dancing on the top floor. He grabbed a pint of cider and watched the packed dance floor. Notwithstanding being engaged to Carol, Ken was extremely shy when it came to the opposite sex and so he was quite surprised when a girl named Jane asked him to dance. It transpired she lived locally with her grandmother and was studying Art at Chester College. Dancing stopped at 11.00 and Ken escorted Jane home, putting a piece of paper with her name and address on into his wallet, before hitch-hiking back to Ellesmere Port.

It was some days later when Ken was joined by Roger who had been working with Stordy's in a factory in Swindon. At one stage they were working together on an oven at the rear of the factory when to their amazement a large ship passed by, the upper half of the ship being visible as it glided past with smoke pouring out of its single funnel. Neither of them had realized that the Manchester Ship Canal was directly behind the factory! The following Saturday, Ken talked Roger into taking a bus into Chester with him and they made their way again to Dixie Dean's bar. Dixie Dean had been a famous football player for Everton and had an amazing scoring record, including a record sixty league and FA cup goals in a single season. Ken's aim was to go onto Quaintways with Roger, who declined and made his way back to Ellesmere Port, Ken soon following.

Employment with Stordy's ended for Ken after the Ellesmere Port job, since he had to get ready for a return to College and take up his scholarship. He also had to work through a small research-based text by the Cambridge Mathematician A.E. Ingham and did so by going each day to the quiet study room at Wolverhampton Library. Whilst back at home, he would either sleep on a bed settee in the lounge, sharing it with Reg if and when he was at home, or he would sleep on a settee at Carol's. A serious family row broke out one Saturday when Reg was home, Ken and his siblings criticizing Reg in very strong language about not ensuring money was sent to Norma each week and also not enough money when he did send a registered letter. Reg made a feeble excuse and made a statement about how much he earned, Ken immediately calling him a liar, since he had been earning twice as much at Stordy's as Reg had claimed. There followed an altercation, Reg punching Ken who did not retaliate, Keith holding Reg off. Besides spending money on drink, and totally failing in his duty to Norma and his family, there may have been some social factors behind Reg's behaviour: (a) it was still the age when wages were paid in cash and in envelopes with a see-through window, many men immediately going to the pub on receipt of wages, with consequent implications for the amount handed over to wives or family (b) like most working men, Reg did not have a bank account so making access to money difficult for families (c) Reg was on the so-called staff of the company, staff commonly receiving a guaranteed fixed level of wage independent of hours worked. Thus it might be possible for Ken to earn more than the supervising Engineer by working 7 days a week and long hours each day (d) the supervising engineers were paid weekly and expenses were paid weekly in arears. Thus the costs of variable travel and accommodation each week meant that one had to subsidize such expenses initially from wages before retrieving them.

It was now time to return to College and to take up lodgings at the Castle Hotel. Reporting to the Department, Ken he found he was one of six returnees in Pure Mathematics. The other five were to take a Masters' Degree programme, Ken being exempt due to being the only one with First Class Honours and being required to attend the MSc classes but not take exams and to register for a PhD directly. It was an enjoyable time for him and he mixed well with the other students, enjoying learning for learning's sake, rather than for exams, and during breaks he learned how to play bridge.

Besides the MSc classes, he had a weekly one-to-one tutorial with Prof Pennington and was given various small problems within the subject of Divergent Series and number theory, these being linked to papers of the late Prof G. H. Hardy and Pennington's own PhD Supervisor at Cambridge, A.E. Ingham. Ken found Ingham's papers to be deep in difficulty and beautifully elegant, and he had thoughts about applying to Cambridge to continue his PhD. However Ingham sadly died that year and also an opportunity came up to apply for a Tutorship in Mathematics at the College, this being a paid position well in excess of the Scholarship value. Two such tutorships were available and both Ken and Howard Jones, his classmate, were interviewed and appointed from the following September. In the meantime the MSc students took exams at the same time as the undergraduates and then embarked upon a written Dissertation. Unfortunately, the main refectories closed and Ken and his fellow students had to resort to the town for evening meals. Money was short and both he and another classmate, Mike, made use of Joe's fish and chip shop for 15 successive days. They each ordered pie and chips and ate these as they strolled along the seafront towards the bus stop. Dessert followed, consisting of an ice cream bought just before reaching the bus stop. Arriving at the Department the boys made their way to the postgraduate room and drinks facilities, rounding off their three course meal with hot coffee in their individual mugs!

Chapter 6 Transition to an Academic's Life

Ken returned home for a summer break. Having given Carol the news about securing a full-time university position, they decided to marry that summer. Ken needed money however, although his trips with Mike for pie and chips meant he had saved enough from his Scholarship to pay for the wedding reception. In the meantime he resolved to try and get a job for 5 weeks to boost their resources. An opportunity came up as a bus conductor for the Midland Red Bus Company, the position being based at their garage at the bottom of Castle Hill, Dudley. "You need to take this standard test," said William, the Employment Officer, giving Ken the test paper and 1 hour to finish it. "Gee," thought Ken, the questions being all based on simple arithmetic, mirroring what would happen when you had to charge for multiple tickets and give change. He completed the test in 15 minutes. "You passed that easily enough," said William "now go to room 101 on the first floor and have a medical administered by the Company doctor." He went to room 101 and knocked. "Come in," said the Doctor, Ken explaining that he was being hired as a bus conductor subject to a medical. "You look a fit young man. How are you feeling?" said the Doctor. "Fine, no problem." "OK, you have passed," said the Doctor, giving him a grin as he signed a medical form. "Take this back upstairs and you will be ready to start." Ken gave the form to William who said "Well done, you need to be here for 5:30 a.m. tomorrow morning and will start on the 244 route between Cradley Heath and Wednesbury. Here is a ticket machine, a spare roll and a fare schedule, although you will find most people tell you what fare they want. I have assigned you locker 25 in the Conductor's Office. You report there after each shift, cash up and place the day's takings and summary in the shute in there. Be careful to be accurate since if your takings are less than the tally on the machine, the Wages Office will deduct the difference from your wages. If your take is more than the tally, you hand it in to the company. Your driver tomorrow will be George Fellows but do note that the conductor is the manager of the bus," said William. George was a bit of a celebrity but was very reticent about his status, being the father-in-law of Led Zeppelin drummer John Bonham. Ken

57

nodded and made his way home. Fortunately he had Carol's bike and so was able to get to the Bus Garage a few minutes early the next morning, collect his equipment and meet up with George. Off went the bus up Castle Hill to Fisher Street, collected two passengers and made its way towards Great Bridge where three more passengers were waiting. "Sod it," said Ken as his ticket machine jammed. He had no idea what to do. " Gie it here yo," said George in his thick Black Country accent, as he climbed out of the driver's cab of the double decker bus. George took the machine and gave it a bang with his fist, freeing it up. And so the bus went on its way, Ken having no more trouble with the machine and passengers being very kind to him. After a short stop at the Wednesbury terminus, the bus made its way back towards Dudley, Ken just about coping with the big increase in passengers, working men getting off at the various factories on the way. At the same time he managed to cope with both upstairs and downstairs, calling out "tickets please" and finding the passengers very friendly and helpful.

The stage from Dudley to Cradley Heath was new to Ken but on arrival George climbed out and said "We con tek a 20 minute break here," leading him to a little café near the stop, where a lady already had tea and a bacon sandwich ready for George. "What yow want, darling?" said Flo, the lady behind the counter. "The same please," said Ken, displaying the effect on his accent of four years at university. And so the day continued with a break for tea or for lunch with tea occurring every time the Cradley Heath terminus was reached. Ken really enjoyed the camaraderie and the constant interaction with passengers. The shift completed at 1:00 p.m. but William came over and said "We are short this evening, would you like to do an evening shift from 6:00 to 11:00? We pay you overtime at time and a quarter and also pay spread-over time from 1:00 to 6:00." "Thanks, that will be OK," said Ken, mentally totting up the additional pay.

Time passed by quickly but Ken found covering both a morning and evening shift extremely tiring. This was also the case for the drivers. On one occasion, Ken's bus came down Castle Hill on its way to Birmingham, the driver turning right into the Bus Garage and then turning the engine and lights off. Ken jumped off the bus, shouting to the driver who immediately realized what he had done and sheepishly climbed back into his cab. On another occasion, Ken had descended from the bus to help a blind lady off and across the road. However the driver pulled away before Ken had got back on leaving him running after the bus before a passenger knocked the driver's cab to alert him.

Ken was two weeks into the job when a fellow conductor, Frank, noticed that Ken's take was in excess of that recorded on the machine and that he was about to pay in the excess. "We dow do that," said Frank. "These buggers tek shortages owt of yow wages but expect yow to gie em excesses. Dow be saft! None of us gie back excesses so when yome short, yove covered the loss from yow wages." Ken also discovered another wheeze, particularly on the 125 and 126 buses from Dudley to Birmingham. Passengers poured off the buses in Birmingham, particularly workers in the morning, and any still to pay would hand you the fare if you stood on the rear platform as they rushed off the bus. The wheeze was to run off penny tickets for such passengers and throw them to the floor, so ensuring you were not short at cashing up time!

During week three, two further amusing incidents occurred. Ken was to take the 125 bus out at 5:30 a.m. on Monday, but on arriving at the Bus Garage discovered that his driver, Jock the Scotsman, was late. The bus Inspector, Lofty Rhodes, was a tall thin man, very like the character in the television series "On the buses". "And what bloody time do you call this! I'm going to report you and cut your wages this week," said Lofty. Jock was a little the worse for weather, having been drinking on the Sunday evening. He jumped into the cab, cursing Lofty, Ken jumping onto the rear platform, and off they went. Jock went all the way to Birmingham and back without stopping, leaving prospective passengers waving and shouting to him at the stops, and then, as he passed the Bus Garage on the return, Jock put two fingers up to Lofty, who stood there mouth agape, the 125 being now back on schedule!

Thursday saw Ken back on the 244 bus, which, on the way from Cradley to Dudley broke down. George, the driver, pulled into the kerb and informed the passengers of the problem, suggesting they get off the bus and he would call for a replacement. "Yow stay ere and look after the bus," said George. After a few minutes a man of about 30 got onto the bus and sat down, Ken noticing he was wearing underpants but no trousers. "I'm sorry Sir, but the bus has broken down and so you need to get off and make your way to the next stop," said Ken. The passenger looked perplexed but followed the instructions. Some 20 minutes later a man in a white coat jumped onto the bus and asked Ken if he had seen a man without trousers, it transpiring that the man had run away from a mental hospital.

Ken's most embarrassing experience occurred on a local bus when his Aunt Doris was on the upper deck with her friends. The national news had disclosed that the plans for Prince Charles' university education included one year at the University College of Wales, Aberystwyth, in order to prepare for his investiture as Prince of Wales. Doris jumped from her seat as Ken appeared on the top of the stairs. "Listen everyone, here is my nephew Ken who will be at university with Prince Charles. But Prince Charles will only be a student, whereas Ken will be a teacher." "Tickets please," said Ken blushing profusely.

Ken completed his job as a bus conductor in the last week of July and helped Carol with preparations for their wedding. A trip was made to Aberystwyth to finalize their accommodation, they having secured a small furnished flat on the top floor of one of the Victorian terraced houses on the north end of the promenade. There were 84 steps to be climbed to the top floor, the flat comprising a lounge, a small kitchenette, a bathroom and two bedrooms. The lounge and smaller bedroom were at the front of the flat and had sloping ceilings parallel to the roof, this being compensated for by wonderful views of Cardigan Bay, the sea, Constitution Hill, the pier and part of the seafront. Ken and Carol had booked into a hotel in Shrewsbury for the evening of the wedding day, and took the train there a couple of hours after the start of the wedding reception. Having arrived by train and booked into their room, they made their way to the hotel lounge and asked at reception for a cider and a port and lemon. The receptionist turned his nose up, saying firmly "I am afraid not Sir, this is a temperance hotel!" Breakfast the following day was minimal suggesting that the hotel was also one for slimmers!

Ken now embarked upon preparation for his new academic role. The Tutorship involved both teaching a formal class and giving wider tutorial support, Ken also discovering that his registration as a full-time PhD student had now to be changed to part-time, lengthening the minimum time for submission of his thesis but this fitting well with the three year position as Tutor. His fellow Tutor, Howard Jones, had passed the MSc with flying colours and had also registered for a PhD. Howard was a local resident, having gone to Aberystwyth's Ardwyn Grammar School, and he and Ken now shared an office.

Carol had also secured a full-time position in Aberystwyth, starting September 1st, having qualified at Wolverhampton Technical College as a Demonstrator. She was based in the MANWEB (Merseyside and North Wales Electricity Board) showroom and had a variety of roles including demonstrating kitchen and laundry equipment both at the showroom and in customers' homes, giving occasional public cookery demonstrations and travelling to other showrooms in the mid-Wales area. There was no washing machine in the flat, nor any space for one, but Carol had the perk of being able to test washing machines and driers on a Wednesday afternoon when the showroom was closed. The test always included their own weekly washing!

Their flat was owned by a Dr and Mrs Rees, who lived on the second floor and were now retired, Dr Rees having been a family doctor in the town. Mrs Rees was an extremely refined lady and very nice to them. Under the agreement with Dr Rees, rent was to be paid monthly and no changes were to be made to the decoration of the property without his agreement. Ken and Carol had little money after the expense of the wedding and were horrified to find out that both of their jobs involved no pay until the end of the month, i.e. the end of September. They were bailed out by the kindness of Carol's parents who gave them a loan of £50 to see them through. Life in Aberystwyth trundled along, with Carol and Ken having had the unusual experience of family visitors on the first night of their stay in their flat, this lasting throughout the year with almost no break. It seemed not to concern them since both were from large families and were used to living in homes constantly full of parents, siblings and friends.

A small breakthrough in widening their social life occurred when they decided their finances could stretch to acquiring a second hand car, this being a yellow Ford Anglia, only three years old. Carol had previous limited access to a small MANWEB Austin minivan but this could only be used for work purposes and had to be returned each day. Ken had previously had driving lessons in Dudley and failed his test, primarily because of stalling at a traffic lights and also being deemed as not looking in his mirror sufficiently often. There were no traffic lights in Aberystwyth, the nearest being in Welshpool, some 40 miles away. He took his test again after 7 lessons. Apart from a terrific downpour midway through the test, forcing him to pull over and clean the steamed-up window, all went well, even the hill start on the very steep Penglais Hill. Having a car meant that they could explore the area, make frequent visits to nearby Borth and the Ynyslas sand dunes and eat out occasionally at remote restaurants such as Tyn-y-Cornel at Lake Talyllyn in the southern end of the Snowdonia National Park. They would also meet up from time to time for a fish and chips lunch, sitting in the car alongside the harbour, especially during high winds when the white waves would crash over the harbour wall.

Ken's work towards his PhD had developed slowly and centred on routine extensions of certain so-called summability methods, regarded even then as very old fashioned mathematics. A breakthrough did occur in his second year following a problem raised by Prof Pennington. Ken had been tussling with the problem for some months when, as he watched the football review programme, Match of the Day, on the BBC one Saturday night, he suddenly had a burst of inspiration, and worked on this into the early hours of Sunday. The inspirational ideas bore fruit and, having tightened up the proofs involved, Ken presented his new results to Prof Pennington who encouraged him to write them up for publication and to submit the resulting paper to the Proceedings of the Cambridge Philosophical Society. This gave invaluable understanding of the submission process and the enormously helpful confidential refereeing system, Ken's paper being eventually accepted and published.

During his second year, Ken joined Howard in a bridge team of four, playing in the Cardiganshire Bridge League, mainly centred on Aberystwyth. This involved visiting different homes, duplicate bridge being played in two separate rooms and scores on identical hands being compared between the teams. The overall scores were then converted to IMPs (International Match Points) the maximum win being 6 nil. Ken's team included Howard and two young lecturers in Applied Mathematics, all three being excellent players. Ken was very much the beginner, having been taught by Howard and using ACOL, a set of British conventions. However he managed to hold his own and was delighted when his team won the league, thus qualifying for the national championships in Porthcawl, South Wales. The team produced an average performance there but were very upset the following year. It transpired that some way into the season, an influential figure in another team had the Rules changed so that the league would now be decided on total IMPs, not as in football on points for wins, losses and ties. Ken's team had already beaten this person's team and went on to win all of their matches in the season, only to receive runners-up trophies!

In late April, Ken was invited by Dr (later Prof) Ken Walters to join the staff cricket team for a match against the College student team. It was an evening 20-over game and the first time Ken had played since captaining his Grammar School team some 4 years before. The students batted first scoring 125 runs, the staff team then losing wickets rapidly. Ken went in at number 6 and rather than attempt a win, he put his head down and batted through the rest of the innings for 27 not out, much to the annoyance of the student captain. As far as Ken was concerned it was a draw but he was never clear as to the actual result. He was then invited to play regularly for the Staff team who played against local sides, teams from as far as Shrewsbury, as well as in an annual three day tournament hosted by one of the constituent Colleges of the University of Wales. He also made guest appearances for West Bromwich Nomads, who played friendly matches against cricket teams across the Midlands on weekends. The Nomads team mirrored much of the ethnic profile of the Birmingham area with players with heritages from India, Pakistan, the West Indies, and the U.K.

Disaster struck in April of Ken's third year of research, following lunch at the University Staff dining room with Prof Pennington and a visiting speaker, Dr Alan Beardon, at the mathematics seminar series. Returning to the Department, Prof Pennington ran up the staircase and collapsed, subsequently tragically passing away at the very young age of 44, leaving a wife and 4 children, all girls.

It transpired that Prof Pennington had been teaching an Honours course on the subject of Divergent Series, using a text of that title by G. H. Hardy, the subject matter being closely connected with Ken's PhD studies. Following a discussion between senior staff, he was asked if he would complete the 12 classes of the course, set the Honours Exam paper and tutor the students taking the course as they prepared for finals. The task was a bit daunting but he agreed and then met with the students, borrowed the class notes of one of the best of them and set to work. Unlike many other countries, the system of university mathematics teaching in the UK was such that lecturers rarely worked from a single text but drew on a number of texts and papers in putting a course together. Thus each course represented the particular interests of the teacher whilst being based on an outline syllabus. At the same time, there was a principle in the UK that Honours degrees were meant to be of the same standard across universities, and the entire system used a process of external examiners to monitor this. Such people tended to be experts in the field, their appointments were subject to peer scrutiny, they were generally appointed for three to five years, and they were required to have had no direct recent substantial involvement with the university for which they fulfilled the role. Furthermore the number of universities they could simultaneously act for was limited, often to at most three, but the system did then provide continuous cross fertilization and maintenance of standards. Following exams, the external would receive sample papers and would visit the university to check papers, meet with lecturers to discuss issues and sit on the final exam board that decided upon passes, fails and Honours classifications.

Having checked student notes and the outline syllabus, Ken was quite reasonably able to construct the final 12 lectures. The exam paper and mark scheme presented a difficult challenge since there were no previous papers to rely upon, but he was able to draft a paper using the standard *theorem plus associated rider* approach used at that time in most subjects in Mathematics. His draft exam paper was sent off to the external examiner, Prof B. Kuttner of Birmingham University, Ken being relieved to receive feedback that the standard was acceptable with no issues. Indeed in the summer exams, the students performed in line with expectations and performances in other mathematics subjects. However Ken was brought down to earth when he found out that Prof Kuttner, an internationally recognised expert in the field, had thought the paper had been set by Prof Pennington and consequently had not pursued any isssues.

Ken again played cricket for the University Staff team during the summer and also helped to arrange a three day tour by West Bromwich Nomads, the schedule involving matches against the University Staff, Aberystwyth Town and the nearby village of Llanilar. The match against the University was played on the University's excellent cricket ground and ran over three sessions starting at 11:00 a.m. Accommodation was arranged in new buildings at the top of Penglais Hill, these containing self-catering units hosting up to four or six persons. The Nomads arrived in cars and with a coach containing supporters, some 60 of whom then watched from the covered stand and kept up a barrage of music and banter. The game started on time with the lunch break set for 1:00 p.m. by which time the Nomads had collapsed to 65 for 6 wickets. One of the features of the West Indian players was their attacking style of cricket, unlike the dour batting of the English players who were brought up on the importance of the forward defensive stroke.

Following lunch, two of the Nomads West Indian batsmen ran riot, hitting the ball to all parts of the ground with the team eventually being all out for 190 runs mid-way through the afternoon session. The University team were then exposed to the fast bowling of the Nomads and were eventually all out for 125 runs after the tea interval and 45 minutes before the allotted close of play. A successful start to their tour but little did anyone realize that this fixture and tour would continue for the next 20 years!

During that summer, Ken continued to work on his PhD and investigated the summability method of Ingham and some related issues in number theory. He also came across papers by Dr I. J. Maddox, a former PhD student of Prof Kuttner and former lecturer at Birmingham University. The University of Wales had appointed Dr Alun Morris, a lecturer in the Department, to the Chair of Pure Mathematics and Head of Department. Prof Morris interviewed Ken about progress on his PhD and whether he could suggest anyone who might take on the supervision. He suggested Dr Maddox, now Reader at Lancaster University, Prof Morris writing to Dr Maddox who kindly accepted the role.

Ken travelled to Lancaster in the Ford Anglia, leaving the M6 motorway just prior to the city. As he moved off a roundabout at the junction the bonnet of the car suddenly shot into the air, Ken immediately pulling up and closing the bonnet. Dr Maddox had arranged for him to stay for a week in a visitors' room on the top of a hall of residence. On settling in and then making his way to the Department, he was met by one of Dr Maddox's PhD students, Constantine Lascarides from Greece. Constantine then introduced him to Dr Maddox who quizzed him about his background, gave him a copy of a pre-publication of a paper entitled *Tauberian Constants* and spent two hours each day talking to him about his current research and ideas for development. Maddox's pre-paper involved both classical summability and use of the current in-vogue and relatively modern subject of Functional Analysis. Ken was grateful that he had attended a voluntary set of graduate lectures on Functional Analysis given by a new young lecturer at Aberystwyth. After returning to Aberystwyth, he worked intensively and achieved a considerable breakthrough, applying Maddox's results to number theoretic applications, establishing links with the famous Prime Number Theorem, and extending the theory of Tauberian Constants to new areas.

Now about to enter his final year of the Tutorship, and needing quiet study time to begin writing his thesis, he and Carol decided to rent a furnished cottage at Cefyn Clwyd, a tiny hamlet in the hills some five miles east of Aberystwyth. There were two downstairs rooms, an upstairs bedroom with a sloping ceiling, an open fireplace and a kitchenette but no bathroom and no hot water. The toilet was outside in the garden and had no light. Carol's workmate Bill, an electrician, came to the rescue and, with the owners' permission, rewired the cottage and installed a water heater in the kitchenette. They again attracted family visitors from time to time but nowhere near the same numbers as before. The rent was 40% lower than the seafront flat and notwithstanding the rustic conditions, provided the quietness sought by Ken when he started writing his thesis.

He made a second trip to see Dr Maddox at Lancaster University, a curious event occurring as he left the M6 just short of the town. At exactly the same roundabout as on the previous visit, the bonnet of the Ford Anglia again flew open! (This never happened again anywhere during his ownership of the vehicle.) The visit proved extremely useful in closing some of the gaps in Ken's work and giving ideas to extend the later chapters.

Regarding relaxation, he continued to play bridge and near Christmas also joined the owners of the cottage, Mr and Mrs Jones, in a whist drive at the nearby village of Penryncoch. Some 200 people were present and it seemed that everyone was speaking Welsh. To his surprise he finished joint first and was called up to the stage with the other winner to draw a card to determine who would get first prize and who would get second. He lost the draw, the winner receiving a turkey whilst Ken was presented with a pair of coat hangers!

For the last three years he had played centre forward for the College Staff team in the Aberystwyth & District League and was elected as captain for his final year. When the last match of the season approached, both Staff and their opponents, Padarn, had won all of their matches, Padarn having a superior goal average. The match was heading for a nil-nil tie when Ken was brought down in the penalty area, Staff being awarded a penalty by the referee. Ken was the regular penalty taker and as usual hit the ball in the left hand corner of the net, his team winning by the only goal. When Staff were awarded the Championship Shield one week later, he proudly took the trophy to the Staff Common Room to display it there but was met with little enthusiasm from the non-footballing lecturers and Professors!

This was the year in which Prince Charles attended the University College of Wales, Aberystwyth, in preparation for his investiture. Ken and colleagues had been briefed to treat Prince Charles as any other student. However it was rumoured that he had arrived by helicopter and had a red carpet outside his room in the Hall (just like any other student?). Prince Charles was sometimes seen around town with his friend, David Frost, sharing a small red sports car. It gave Ken a good but largely false story to tell over the years. True, they had parked in the car park to the Mathematics Department as Ken walked out. He claimed: I went across and said "Hey you cannot park there. This is for Jukes (Dukes) not Princes!"

Ken made a final visit to Lancaster, taking with him an outline contents page of his proposed thesis and his latest results linking Tauberian Constants and Analytic Number Theory. At the end of a 2 hour review he asked "Do you think I should proceed to write up now Prof Maddox?" "Yes, go ahead and send me the draft chapters as you proceed," was the reply. So he returned to the cottage and began the arduous task of writing up. At the same time he began scouring the Times Higher Educational Supplement for possible jobs in mathematics in universities, applying in the Spring for one at Bangor and another at Queen's University, Belfast. Interviews were offered at both but the visit to Bangor was extremely disappointing. Ken was taken to lunch with another candidate by one of the Mathematics Senior Lecturers, Dr Brown, who Ken then discovered was standing in at short notice for the Head of Department who had been taken ill. "And what aspects of topology are you working on for your PhD?" asked Dr Brown. "I'm not into topology. I'm into Classical and Functional Analysis with applications to Analytic Number Theory," replied Ken. Dr Brown looked very puzzled, saying "But the Department needs a topologist, I'm not sure what you are doing here." The conversation fizzled out and after lunch interviews took place, Dr Brown being on the panel. Ken was not offered the position!

Chapter 7 Northern Ireland 1969-72

Ken's second interview was in May 1969 at Queen's University, Belfast, where the Head of Department Prof Samuel Verblunsky was also a specialist in mathematical analysis. Ken was quite excited to be flying for the first time, driving to Liverpool Speke airport from which there was a direct flight on a very small plane to Belfast. Queen's University seemed very grand, the main campus being on the Malone Road and the Pure Mathematics Department being housed in the left wing of the main building with views across lush green manicured lawns and beautiful flower beds. After a briefing by Personnel and a Senior Lecturer in Mathematics, Ken was taken through the main hall to a waiting room with three other candidates, each being called in turn. He was the third to be interviewed and sat at the end of a long conference table, with a panel of ten including a cleric. This was his first time in Ireland and he had no idea at all of the history of Northern Ireland. After exploring teaching experience and the state of progress of his PhD, the cleric said "Mr Jukes, I see you have a paper published at Cambridge, could you describe exactly what Cesaro Summability is?" Ken's experience of having finished Prof Pennington's course on Divergent Series shone through, another panel member then saying "I read that there was an incident recently in North Wales where a Welsh Nationalist bombed an RAF station. It seems quite a dangerous country, do you agree?" "Not at all sir," said Ken, explaining the normally peaceful nature of Wales. The interview ended with the Chairman asking "Mr Jukes. If we offered you the position would you accept?" Ken said that he would. He would learn later in his career that this question was a standard one in academic appointment procedures.

As was the custom, the panel continued to meet after the final candidate had been interviewed. A panel member then opened the door, "Mr Jukes, this way please" and Ken was delighted to be offered the permanent post of Assistant Lecturer, members of the panel then congratulating him. He phoned Carol with the news and then went to the Bursar's Office to discuss salary and start date and to complete a claim for travel and hotel expenses.

Now back in Wales, Ken and Carol agreed that they would need to make a visit to Belfast to sort out accommodation and banking arrangements. They also made the decision to try to start a family, Carol immediately conceiving! The return trip to Ireland was to be made at their own expense and they decided to take a boat from Liverpool to Belfast. This was an awful experience, making them both seasick and wishing they had flown instead. The University had a flat becoming vacant but it was unfurnished and in extremely poor condition; they opted instead to rent a semi-detached furnished house in a small town called Glengormley on the northern side of Belfast.

The summer months approached, Ken finalizing the write up of his PhD and sending chapters to Dr Maddox, who seemed to be supportive of his writing style and the structure of the thesis. Following the summers exams, he reached agreement with the Department Secretary to type up his thesis for a standard fee, this being typed as usual onto stencils using an electric typewriter with an interchangeable "golf ball" with mathematical symbols. Typos were corrected with Tippex, a common "white-out". There was great relief when the final version was printed out on a duplicating machine and some four additional copies also produced. These were then taken to a shop in the town that specialized in binding student theses, three copies being submitted to the Registrar's Office in the University. It transpired that the University processes led to the appointment of Prof Kuttner as External Examiner, his task as an internationally recognized expert in the field being to read the thesis in detail and then to carry out an oral examination of the PhD candidate.

It was during that summer of 1969 that Ken became more aware of the history and geography of Northern Ireland but things seemed to be relatively peaceful, apart from marches that had taken place with regard to an apparently unfair voting system. One of the leading activists was a young Queen's law student named Bernadette Devlin. Carol and Ken needed to take their Ford Anglia with them and with some trepidation booked themselves and the car onto the ferry from Liverpool. This time the overnight crossing was fairly calm and they duly entered Belfast Lough and the harbour, noticing a pall of smoke rising above a distant row of houses. They were a little perturbed when the car was unloaded, it being winched by a crane from the hold, the wheels being chained to a steel tubular structure. Driving into Belfast towards the University, they were alarmed when the traffic was suddenly stopped by an army unit who threw a barricade across the road and diverted the car. It transpired that the row of houses had been set on fire deliberately. After entering the University and parking in front of the main building, they entered and introduced themselves to Prof Verblunsky who showed Ken his allocated office on the second floor and gave him a teaching timetable. They then went to the Northern Bank opposite the University and opened a joint account, before making their way to Glengormley, some 30 minutes travel from the University. The house there was in the middle of a cul-de-sac on a hill about one mile from the centre of the town, through which ran the Antrim Road, giving access by bus to the centre of Belfast. "Brrr, it's cold here, let's make up a coal fire," said Carol, this being the heating system for the house. This phrase was to be repeated many times over the next few months as they experienced the damp climate and the manner in which cold damp conditions and fine drizzle seemed to penetrate your clothing.

Life in Northern Ireland was a totally new experience for them, the so called "troubles" escalating and making them fully aware of the Protestant-Catholic divide. At the same time there was an opportunity to experience the calm and beauty of the countryside, one of their regular trips being a drive to Carrickfergus and along the Antrim coast road, a stop on the north coast at the Giant's Causeway, and then to Portrush and back through Coleraine towards Belfast. They were always wary of going west of Portrush to Londonderry, since this always seemed to be a hotbed of political unrest. Glengormley seemed to be stable even though there was a mixed population of Catholics and Protestants; indeed this was the case with the neighbours either side of them. Whilst both neighbours spoke to them, but treated them as foreigners rather than British, they did not speak to each other. This was not the case with their children who formed sides, with the Protestants holding dustbin lids, whilst the Catholics attempted to hit them on the legs with all sorts of missiles!

"When is your oral exam due?" said Prof Verblunsky to Ken who replied "it was to be held in November, but the external examiner, Prof Kuttner of Birmingham University, is on a visit to India and is not due back until March." "Keep me informed Mr Jukes and let me know as soon as possible the date. Meantime how are your classes going?" "All seems to be going well Sir, I am just about getting used to the Saturday morning class." In fact this class, which also met on Tuesdays and Thursdays, was quite a challenge even though it was at Level 0. Queen's operated a four year undergraduate programme with Level 0 being the normal entry, entry at Level 1 requiring exceptional A-level performance, many such students having 3 Grade A's. Ken's approach to his courses always involved interaction with his students but the difficulty with two of the students in his Level 0 class was in understanding their broad Belfast accents, leading initially to Ken half guessing what their questions actually were!

Civil unrest continued to develop as the New Year approached and Carol's pregnancy neared its termination. She was admitted to the Royal Victoria Hospital, on the Shankill Road on February 5th but by February 7th had still not delivered. That evening Ken left the University around 7:00 p.m., left his car at the University and was to take a bus to the Hospital. However there had been civil trouble near the Hospital, the bus being cancelled, so he had to walk there. On arrival he was allowed to enter the delivery area, Carol being on a gas and air mixture and being surrounded by some four other stalls. One particular lady was screaming from time to time, whilst the doctor in charge stood by, wearing a white coat and what appeared to be short wellingtons, and was smoking heavily but did not converse with Ken. After a few hours Ken took the lift to a waiting area, and took coffee from a machine. The nurse at the desk said "Mr Jukes, your wife should be delivering in the next 20 minutes but please wait here." It was now the early hours of February 8th, Ken being informed after some 30 minutes that Carol had given birth to a girl, that all was well, but that he would need to come back the next morning before he could see Carol and the baby. He walked from the hospital back to Queen's, collected his car and drove back to Glengormley in a state of euphoria, returning to the hospital the next morning. "How are you feeling?" he asked, holding the baby for the first time. "Still very sore," said Carol as she lifted the blanket back to show a horrific long scar on her belly. Ken was appalled to learn that she had delivered by Caesarian section, totally without his knowledge. He called Carol's parents to give them the news and was delighted to learn that her mother, Floss, was coming over to help. Following Carol's discharge from the hospital, Floss arrived having taken a taxi from the airport. However there had been a heavy snowfall that night and the taxi was unable to get into the cul-de-sac, Ken spotting it from the front window and stepping out into the snow to collect Floss and her case. Floss's help with Carol and her first grandchild was so welcome and also allowed Ken to fulfil his teaching commitments at Queen's. They resolved to name the baby Kerry Joanne, the first name reflecting one of their favourite locations, namely Kerry Forest in Montgomeryshire, Wales.

April soon came around, Ken informing Prof Verblunsky that his PhD oral was to take place at Birmingham University later that month. He travelled to Carol's parents' home in Tipton and borrowed an old car, travelling in it the next day and making his way to Prof Kuttner's office in the Mathematics Department for a 10:00 a.m. start. "Come in," said Prof Kuttner as Ken knocked the door, finding that Dr Maddox and Prof Morris were also present. Prof Morris was there to represent the University of Wales and to see fair play, the oral being led by Prof Kuttner, who proceeded to point out some redundancy in one of the earlier chapters but then focussed on the chapters on Tauberian Constants. Ken was given a real, very detailed but positive grilling over some three hours. It was Dr Maddox who widened the discussion outside of the thesis with some piercing and deep questions. Ken was then required to withdraw from the room, being called back in some 15 minutes later, to be told by Prof Morris that he had passed the oral examination and PhD. Congratulations were given by the panel and Ken was mightily relieved. It transpired that though no-one had taken lunch, both Prof Morris and Dr Maddox realized that they could just about catch trains back home. Ken offered them a lift to New Street station which they gratefully accepted, only to find that the battery on his car had failed and a push start was required. So the event finished with Prof Morris and Dr Maddox pushing the car which duly started, Ken then dropping them off at the station!

"How did the oral go?" asked Prof Verblunsky on Ken's arrival the next morning, congratulating him on hearing the good news and then saying "I would like you to give a new Honours option next year based on your research topic." Ken was happy to be asked, and informed Prof Verblunsky of the title so as to include it in the options for next academic year. He decided to base part of the course on Dr Maddox's textbook *"Elements of Functional Analysis,"* the students having covered point set topology and metric spaces in Level 2 and taking a full course in Functional Analysis in Level 3. Ken had already worked through the textbook, doing all of the exercises at the end of the chapters and informing Lascarides and Dr Maddox of possible errors and typos. Good news came later in the month when Prof Verblunsky informed Ken that he had been promoted to Lecturer in Pure Mathematics with tenure, the rise in status being accompanied by one extra increment on the salary scale.

Ken was returning to Glengormley by bus one evening and was sitting downstairs on the left hand side by the window alongside a middle aged lady. As he passed the shops in the centre of Belfast, he was suddenly aware of a truck coming up on the inside and was immediately concerned that the space was insufficient, throwing himself sideways across the lady and being covered with glass as the truck took out the side windows of the bus. He later thought "but what if the truck had not taken out the windows!"

The added security of the job led to Carol and Ken considering whether to purchase a house, but the increasing escalation of the "Troubles" was a major concern. "Let's buy one near the border," said Ken to Carol, "then if there is a danger to us, we can more easily cross to safety in Eire." Little did he realize that the border area was one of the most dangerous, members of the IRA apparently carrying out raids via a myriad of narrow lanes across the border, very difficult to man or patrol. After much deliberation they decided to purchase a home and found a new development of some 14 houses in a cul-de-sac in a triangular plot of land in the village of Carryduff, some 6 miles south of Belfast, at the fork of the Saintfield and Ballynahinch roads. Each property consisted of a pair of 3 bedroom semi-detached bungalows with tiny front and rear gardens and an integral garage. They were being built by a private family company and Ken was very impressed with the care taken by the builders and the quality of the construction. They were also pleased with the open countryside, the easy access to Queen's, the simple walk to food stores along the base of the triangle, and the existence of a primary school opposite the stores. The price of the property was £2900 and the quandary was that one could purchase a new detached bungalow for £3300 a half mile away on a recently built estate. But the additional £400 seemed totally unattainable given Ken's salary of £1200 per year and the fact that they had no capital. There was a saving grace in that the University had a special arrangement with an English Building Society, under which they guaranteed 100% mortgages to young lecturers.

They signed up to purchase a home, with the conveyancing being carried out by L'Estrange & Brett, a highly reputable Belfast company recommended by the University, and then had a remarkable piece of good fortune. A cheque was sent by the Building Society to L'Estrange & Brett, with Ken and Carol then to complete the purchase of the property on the following Monday morning. However the Northern Ireland government announced that weekend the provision of a subsidy of £250 per unit to encourage new building, so when they arrived at L'Estrange & Brett they not only completed the purchase but received a refund of £250! This enabled them to buy a new suite of furniture, so they now had a new centrally heated home, a bed, a cot, cutlery, furniture, a TV and a few kitchen implements. Unfortunately there were no built in wardrobes for their clothes but they did have a cupboard below the stairs with coat-hangers.

An opportunity came along before the summer break to assist in the marking of GCE O-level mathematics examinations, Queen's staff being entrusted to the marking, being a non-denominational institution. Carol and Kerry returned to Carol's parents' home in England for the summer. After marking a designated set of scripts to a strict marking scheme Ken was given approval by the Chief Examiner to proceed to the marking of some 500 scripts. He got up each day at 6:00 a.m. and worked through to 11:00 p.m. taking short breaks for innumerable cups of tea and coffee and a staple diet of omelettes with bread and butter. The task was mind numbing and very poorly paid but the additional income was a god-send. Having completed the task in three weeks, he said goodbye to his neighbours and set off to catch the day-time British Rail ferry from Belfast to Heysham in Lancashire.

It was a sunny day but the sea had quite a swell and there were only about thirty passengers on board, all being allowed the use of a cabin below. Ken left the notes for his new Honours course in his briefcase in his cabin and strolled on the deck. As they approached the English coastline there was a sudden commotion, a nearby fishing trawler being on fire. The captain of the ferry tried to come alongside but the two ships were in danger of colliding. A fellow female passenger holding a small baby screamed for the ferry captain to pull away. Ken momentarily could only think of the new course he had spent weeks preparing and so dashed down to collect his briefcase from the cabin and place it in view on the deck, then helping the crew. Every time the crew managed to pass a hose to the trawler the swell of the sea separated it, the wind continuing to fan the flames. Eventually ropes from the ferry were tied to the trawler, the ferry acting as a tug to change the trawler's direction and minimize the effects of the wind. Rescue boats had now arrived from the English ports and were spraying the trawler with water, the ferry eventually disconnecting and making its way to Heysham. Ken and his fellow passengers then boarded a train to nearby Morecombe but the train could only creep along, its brakes having locked up! By this time the connecting train to Birmingham had been missed by some hours, passengers being advised by the station announcer to board the London train to Rugby, this going on the Lichfield route bypassing Birmingham. It was almost 2:00 a.m. when Ken arrived at Rugby and boarded a train back northwards to Birmingham. A fellow passenger asked him "Have you also been to one of the London shows?" but he was too tired to respond about his actual journey! He also found out later that sadly, some five fishermen had died in the fire on the trawler.

In the following academic year, the family settled into life in Northern Ireland and particularly enjoyed the opportunity to drive to the nearby seaside town of Bangor, to the beauty of Strangford Lough and south to the mountains of Mourne. Unfortunately the "Troubles" increased in severity, with many incidents between the Catholic and Protestant communities and between the British Armed Forces and the IRA. On one particular afternoon as Ken was delivering a lecture to the Honours Class, there was an enormous explosion from between the University and City Centre, the class being confronted with scenes of a huge factory fire, the flames rising well above the surrounding buildings way up into the sky. As had become customary, the class showed no panic, the lecture continuing as normal.

Later in the year, Ken and three colleagues volunteered to move out of their offices on the front of Queen's to a house around the corner from a row of Georgian properties owned by Queen's and lying opposite the main building. Each of the four academics, all having Doctorates, were given their own individual rooms, all with their titles displayed on their doors. A fifth room was available for refreshments. The building had previously been a medical facility used by podiatrists and for some three months Ken would get knocks on the door, members of the general public entering and asking him if he could examine their feet!

It was during this time that Ken was away for two days, giving a lecture on his research to the Department of Mathematics at Birmingham University. He was hosted after the talk for dinner at a local Chinese restaurant. As the party watched the news, Ken was shocked to see that a car bomb had exploded outside his new office, breaking windows and taking the entrance door off its hinges!

One of the curious things about the people of Northern Ireland was that they seemed to look towards America rather than the ties to

England. Ken himself had aspirations in this direction and called Prof Morris who had spent a year just a short time ago at the University of Illinois, Champaign Urbana. Following Prof Morris's advice, Ken sent off a CV and letter of application to Illinois and to Lehigh University, Pennsylvania. He was very excited to receive offers from both, the salary at Illinois being $10,000 tax free, $2,000 less than that at Lehigh, but the former was for 9 months, the latter 12 months. Illinois was a huge university, more prestigious than Lehigh, and very famous in many subjects, including number theory in mathematics. After much thought, and after receiving approval from Queen's, he decided to accept the position of Visiting Lecturer at Illinois. Queen's University was extremely generous, covering not only his travel costs but also continuing to pay into the university's pension scheme during his secondment. Having received the offer letter from Illinois, he made his way to the railway station alongside the Belfast Europa hotel in order to secure a passport sized photo. As he walked back outside the station a bomb exploded, showering him with dust; a close call!

He also discovered from the Students Union that he could apply for a position of Academic Group Leader for USIT (the University Students of Ireland Travel organization), this being successful and giving him and his family preferential return air fares to the States and an overnight stay in New York City. Medical insurance was to be covered through the University of Illinois whilst the combination of their Northern Ireland Driving Licences (which included photo IDs) and International Driving Licences allowed both Carol and Ken to drive in the States.

A curious event occurred towards the end of the academic year, Prof Verblunsky having announced his retirement and a search for a replacement Professor and Head of Department being conducted by Queen's University. It was lunchtime when Ken, walking at the front of the main building, spotted Dr Maddox walking with a group, it transpiring that interviews for the vacancy were taking place. It was later announced that Dr Maddox had been appointed to the Chair of Pure Mathematics! Prof Maddox subsequently came over to seek housing for his family of four but did not bring his wife Irene with him. He stayed with Carol and Ken who transported him to view various properties, Carol acting as Dr Maddox's surrogate wife for the viewings! Irene's brief had been a four bedroom home but Prof Maddox settled on a large three bedroom home in Holywood, just outside Belfast, the house also having a splendid rear garden with outstanding views over Belfast Lough.

Chapter 8 A Year at the University of Illinois

September 1st duly arrived and the family took the train to Dublin where Ken was to meet up with his USIT group at the airport. Arriving at Dublin airport there was no sign of USIT but there was a party of some 20 priests taking the same flight! The family boarded the Aer Lingus flight to JFK Airport, where they were met by USIT personnel and taken by coach to a hotel opposite the Waldorf Astoria. Ken was wearing a heavy winter overcoat to help reduce the weight of their two cases, the Commissionaire at the hotel jokingly asking him if he had flown in from the Arctic, it being over 85°F! This was the first time abroad for both Carol and Ken and they were hesitant to make their way down to breakfast the next morning. They were also hesitant about paying in dollars, not yet understanding the currency and coinage. Plucking up courage, they made it through breakfast and then took a limousine to La Guardia airport where they boarded a flight with Ozark Airlines to Champaign Urbana. The family had been allocated a top floor university apartment in Orchard Downs on the south east corner of the campus, the buildings all being two storeys. However they had not understood the concept of "furnished" in the States. They took a taxi to Orchard Downs, picked a key up at the administration office and walked to the apartment. "Goodness gracious," said Carol "there are no blankets, sheets, pillow cases, TV, cutlery or crockery!" Neither was there any air conditioning, the family sleeping that night on the bare beds and using coats to cover themselves as the air cooled.

There was a service bus between Orchard Downs and downtown, the family making their way next morning to the First National Bank and opening a checking account. An Ace hardware store was nearby, Carol purchasing a minimal set of crockery and cutlery and making do for the time being without sheets or bedding. They also purchased a minimal supply of food from a store called Krogers and travelled back on the bus. Ken made his way the next morning to the Department of Mathematics. Little did he realize just how far and energy sapping it was in the heat as he walked through experimental crop fields and passed the football stadium. He was introduced to the Department Chair, Prof Paul Bateman, the internationally known number theorist, who was dressed casually in slacks and an open collar short-sleeved white shirt. "Come in Dr Jukes, how was your journey here?" said Prof Bateman. "Very good Sir but we are finding the heat a little getting used to. We are staying at Orchard Downs." "And how are you off for cash to get settled down? Would it help to have a $500 advance on your salary? You can pay it off in equal instalments over the year." "It certainly would Sir, thanks very much indeed." "You will be sharing an office with Prof Jerry Uhl. I know he is in so let me take you to meet him." Off they went to meet Jerry, an effervescent character who welcomed Ken, Prof Bateman leaving them to it. "Do you have a car yet since you will definitely need one?" said Jerry. "No, but the American cars are so huge! I have seen a Dodge Dart that would be more in line with my style. Also I can only afford about $500." "Well let's go and look at car lots, we can go round in mine." So off they went, many of the lots being on a single road going south out of town, a single track railway line running alongside the road. There was however no sign of a Dodge Dart, but there were quite a number of Chevrolet Plymouths and Chevrolet Impalas. "Let's take a break for lunch at Walt's Fish Bar where there should be some of the Math Faculty," said Jerry. Entering the bar from the brilliant sunlight gave the impression of total blackness inside but after a few seconds Ken's eyes adjusted and he could see a table in the distance, lit by an overhead lamp, and around which sat 8 people, all men. "Hi all, this here is Dr Ken Jukes, a visiting Professor from Queen's, Ireland." Ken was to get used to being called Professor by academics and students, the title of Dr however being the most important. He later discovered that even some high school teachers used the title Professor; no one referred to the title Lecturer. One of the group called the barman over, asking for two more pitchers of beer, these being shared around. "Ken is looking for a Dodge Dart, does anyone know of any?" said Jerry. All but one shook their heads. "My wife Denise has one, I'll give her a call," said a Dr Phil Green, moving to the phone at the bar and then calling Ken over, saying quietly "she says you can have hers but that I will need to get her a replacement first; she wants a Mercedes convertible sports car. How much do you have in cash?" "I am afraid only about $300." "OK, you can have it for $250, the car is in very good condition, is 3 years old and the mileage is not bad. Let's go since we will have to pick Denise up to get a new car, then to a notary for you to receive the title to the Dodge Dart. Oh, we also need to get you insurance." Denise was waiting outside Altgeld Hall, Ken learning later that she was a Senior Administrator at the University and that Dr Green and she were relatively rich, money being no object.

It took about an hour for Dr and Mrs Green to complete the purchase of a new Mercedes, and he then took Ken to a notary, who witnessed the assignment of the title. Denise had recommended Aetna insurance and so Dr Green took Ken to the Aetna office, all of the staff being female. Fully comprehensive insurance at a very reasonable rate was sorted out, the insurance cover also extending to driving in Canada. It was all rather a whirlwind, but Ken was really grateful. Denise had given the keys of the Dodge Dart to her husband and Dr Green then said "I'll drop you over to the Admin Car Park to pick up the Dodge and you can then drive home." The Dodge was light blue with a bench seat at the front and a huge trunk (boot). Ken said thanks and goodbye to Dr Green and climbed in. The car was a *stick shift*, with the gear lever on the steering wheel and had three gears and a reverse. Ken looked at his watch and realized it was just past 4:00 p.m. People were streaming from the buildings and the traffic level had risen considerably. Ken had never driven on the right hand side but knew that Orchard Downs was on the south east corner of the town, the entire road system being on a rectangular grid design. He decided to wait until the traffic had died down and left the car park at 5:00 p.m., gradually working his way via a sequence of right angled turns and then pulling into the extensive Orchard Downs parking lot near his apartment. He ambled up the stairs and entered the apartment. "Hello, I'm back," said Ken and blurted out the events of his day. Carol was astonished to hear that they now had a car. "Let's go and make our way to Kmart and get the stuff we need."

He studied the local map and drove confidently towards the northwest corner of Champaign, darkness suddenly descending much earlier than in Ireland. The speed limits never exceeded 30 mph, traffic was very light, and drivers seemed to be extremely orderly and careful. He made a right turn and after about 100 yards became alarmed as a car from the opposite direction moved slowly into his side of the road, both cars stopping a few yards apart. The driver of the other car got out and said calmly "You need to turn around, you are in a one-way street." "Thanks, we did not see a sign," said Ken, mightily relieved, the other driver returning to his car and leaving as Ken did a U-turn. He later realized that one-way signs in Champaign Urbana were displayed on the far side of the road, not the near side, as you made a turn. Kmart seemed absolutely gigantic and cheap, but most of the products seemed to have "Made in Hong Kong" or "Made in China" labels. Carol got everything required for the apartment, some toys for Kerry, and splashed out on a TV, no licence being required in Illinois.

The family soon settled in but continued to find the heat and humidity very difficult to adjust to. Meanwhile Ken received his teaching program, including first year courses in Calculus and Linear Algebra and a service course for engineers in Complex Variable. The Math Department seemed to operate the policy of their internal courses all being restricted to a maximum of 30 students but service courses could be much larger. Besides teaching and office hours for individual tutorials, faculty were also expected to contribute to the program of seminars in a wide range of research groups. Ken decided to participate in the number theory group, this involving two faculty seminars and one research student seminar per week. They took place just after mid-day and had an informal atmosphere, participants bringing in food and drinks and contributing ideas to the speaker, including ensuring that all details were worked through.

Carol would normally drive into the University and drop Ken off at Altgeld Hall, the bus also taking the same route from Orchard Downs and so providing an alternative. She joined a family group at the Orchard Downs social centre and made friends with a student couple from Brazil and their children. Ken and Carol also signed up for a group that focussed on ensuring international faculty and students were matched up with American counterparts who would socialize with them and ensure they were not alone at Thanksgiving or Christmas. It transpired that the Jukes were chosen by a couple named Dennie and Peggy Malone (and their dog Puppo), Dennie being a mature student who had served seven years in the US Navy on Polaris submarines, based in Holy Loch, Scotland. Peggy had a Masters degree in English and worked in local Government. The relationship started with an invitation to dinner by Dennie and Peggy to their rented duplex in Champaign, dinner being followed by a game of Monopoly, using the American version. The relationship went very well, neither party realizing that this friendship would be lifelong. The Malone's air conditioning system included windows based units, Ken deciding to try and get one for the Orchard Downs apartment.

It was early October when Carol noticed a "For Sale – air conditioning unit" advert in the Orchard Downs social centre. Ken went to see the unit and decided to purchase it. A ladder was borrowed from the maintenance team and Dennie and Ken proceeded to fit the unit in the window. The improvement in comfort for the family was immediate, Dennie and Peggie being astonished however when the a/c was still kept on at the end of October.

Ken's turn to address the number theory group came in late October, the title of his talk being published as *Arithmetical Summation Methods*. This attracted a full house but it was clear that many of the audience had not appreciated the nature of the content and few came to the continuation talk in the second seminar of the week. Later came an opportunity to speak at the Illinois Number Theory Conference, the international audience including the famous Hungarian Mathematician, Paul Erdos. The Conference was hosted by Illinois State University, Ken sitting behind Prof Erdos in the audience. His talk was about a conjecture connected with Erdos, by Sanford L. Segal of Rochester University. Ken had solved the conjecture and had submitted a paper on his solution to the Journal of the London Mathematical Society. His talk went well but the wind was taken out of his sails in question time, a member of the audience pointing out that Segal himself had published a proof just that week. Ken could not comment but on returning to the library at

Illinois, he went to the New Journals display and found Segal's paper, then sat down to study Segal's quite different approach. He was puzzled by what seemed to be an elementary assertion by Segal within the detail and after a few minutes had shown the assertion to be false, so invalidating Segal's proof. He then wrote a note about the error and sent it to the Journal who published Ken's note as an Erratum and also his full paper and proof.

Thanksgiving soon arrived, being the fourth Thursday of November, the Malones inviting the family to join them in a trip to Dennie's parents' home on the border of Indiana and Illinois, some 10 miles west of Terra Haute. Dennie was the eldest of six children, the others being Maureen (married to a local store manager named Greg), John (who was away in the Navy), Shannon, Kim and Laurie. Their mother Rosie and father Pete lived with the family on a small farm of some 100 acres, Pete supplementing the family income by working in a factory in Terra Haute. The Jukes family were made extremely welcome and sat down at a large table to enjoy the traditional Thanksgiving dinner. The only thing they found unusual was the presence of fruit salad as part of the main course rather than dessert. After the dinner, the children all gathered around a fire in the field next to the house and enjoyed marshmallows pierced by long twigs and toasted on the fire.

Winter arrived with a blast immediately after Thanksgiving, the temperature dropping to around 10°F but with the sun shining brightly. New tenants had arrived in the apartment below and they proved to be very noisy and unfriendly, ignoring Ken's complaints and continuously playing loud music, often with continuous drumming. Following Dennie's advice, Carol and Ken resolved to move and started to look in the local paper and on noticeboards. A 6 bedroom furnished house was advertised in Pennsylvania Avenue, the owner being an academic who was to spend the Spring on sabbatical in Europe. The rent was very reasonable and Carol and Ken called, visited the house in an upmarket area of Urbana and agreed to rent from January 1st.

It was the first week of December when the family experienced their first ice storm. The roads and sidewalks were sheets of ice and the windscreens of cars parked in the open at Orchard Downs had coverings of one to two inches of ice. The branches of the trees were beautiful, glistening with the covering of ice, but were a bit of a menace since the weight of the ice brought some of them crashing down with little warning. "Philip," said Ken to his neighbour "how do you get the ice off the windscreen? Clearly it is no use trying a defroster and it will take ages to clear by running the engine and heater." Philip replied "Just get a couple of buckets of boiling water, throw them on the windscreen and use an ice scraper. Everyone does unless they have a plug-in heater pole; it won't crack the windscreen." So Ken proceeded with some concern to take the advice and was amazed that the method worked without any problems.

Christmas came, there being no Boxing Day as in the UK, and the break was just three days long. Ken's tax free salary of $10,000 for the 9 months, compared with his salary at Queen's of the equivalent of $3365 per year, led to the family being relatively well off and they enjoyed the break, spending Christmas day at Dennie's parents' farm near Terra Haute. Early on January 1st they started to take their belongings over to Pennsylvania Avenue but were shocked on entering the house to find that the owners had left without putting their personal things away. Further, the kitchen was covered with half eaten breakfast food, dirty dishes and dirty cutlery. Carol burst into tears and sat down on the stairs saying "What shall we do?" The owners had run out of time and had rushed to the airport leaving the mess behind. At that moment there was a knock on the door, Mrs Delray, the next door neighbour introducing herself and welcoming them. She was also shocked to see the state of the house and called her husband over. Mrs Delray then took control of the situation, telling them to return to their apartment and saying she would call them when the situation was sorted out. It transpired that she arranged cleaners to come immediately, all personal effects and personal papers being stored away, and the bill sent to the owners! Carol and Ken were called and returned to an amazing transformation.

Living in Urbana was a pleasant experience, helped by the developing friendship with the Malones, the sound bank balance, and with Carol having been able to place Kerry at the age of three in a nearby Kindergarten. The Easter break approached and the winter weather relented. They decided to use the break to take a trip east to Niagara Falls. All went well with the Dodge and they were thrilled with the sight of the Falls on both the American and Canadian sides. They also took the opportunity on the Canadian side to don the voluminous black wet suits and descend the steps to caves behind the waterfall, a truly magnificent experience. On the return journey, they ventured into Michigan, travelling and staying alongside Lake Michigan and having breakfast in Great Falls on Easter Sunday morning.

As the end of semester approached, Ken was asked if he would like to teach "summer school" it being unlikely that he could secure a research grant from the National Science Foundation. Following each course during the year, students completed a questionnaire about the teacher's performance, the results being collated and published internally by the Administration and affecting issues such as tenure and contract continuation. Ken was pleased to come in the top 10% of the rankings and was offered a 2 month summer contract, with his classes being for two sessions of four weeks and running from 7:00 to 10:00 each morning. The conclusion of the rental of the home in Urbana was solved when they were offered the rental of a brick house in Champaign for the summer, the house being beautifully furnished and having a room in the basement that served as a study.

The family moved into their third US rental home at the end of the second semester and decided to take a trip out west, the aim being to see the Grand Canyon, some 1400 miles from Champaign Urbana. A benefit of their membership of the AAA was the provision of maps, including a splendid booklet of "daily" maps giving details of each section of their journey, including distances and guidelines about travel times. As they approached St Louis, Missouri, the Dodge's water temperature indicator started to oscillate sharply. Ken came off the interstate and pulled into a small workshop advertising auto repairs. A kindly gentleman and his wife came out of their adjoining home, fixed the problem, charged a very small amount and wished the family a safe trip. Their first sightseeing stop was at the Meramec Caves in Missouri, these giving a splendid experience of an underground lake, stalactites and stalagmites (tights come down, mites grow up!). An added bonus was the connection of Meramec Caves with the Jesse James gang whom the historical account claimed had a hideout in the caves, old metal chests and statues being exhibited there.

After staying overnight in a roadside motel, the family continued along the old Route 66, sections of which were now interstate and which took them through Oklahoma City, their next overnight stop being in the Texas panhandle, near Amarillo. Here they pulled off the interstate onto a state road that ran north through flat open grassland, a motel with a restaurant opposite being the only buildings in view and about four miles north of the interstate. They booked in and walked across the narrow state road just as two cowboys approached the restaurant from the open range. The cowboys hooked their horses to a wooden rail and entered the restaurant; a true western experience enhanced by the enormous steaks served up for the evening meal.

And so to Albuquerque, New Mexico, where the pornographic film "Deep Throat" was being heavily advertised. Lunch was taken next day at a small town called Gallup, its fame being a claimed invention of the Gallup poll. Whilst the family had gradually acclimatized to the changes in temperature, it was now getting very warm, especially since the Dodge Dart had no air conditioning. It did have two small covers below the dashboard which opened up to give a stream of air, these having to be closed when pulling off onto dirt roads.

New Mexico was hot and dusty with desert like vegetation. "Thank goodness for the cooler and for the availability of ice at the motels," said Carol, the family taking a supply of water and Coca-Cola with them each day. "Let's pull off into the Painted Desert," said Ken. The geology and colours were amazing and the ground around the dirt car park contained lots of petrified logs, these having been originally from trees that had at some stage been buried and soaked in water. The trees took in minerals and changed into stone, these breaking and being exposed when the earth rose up in some far off era. One could have picked up and taken away some of the petrified logs and pieces, a practice which was later banned.

The family aimed next day for Flagstaff, Arizona, the scenery changing with many examples of narrow sections of peninsulas of high land (buttes). They then headed north from Flagstaff to the Grand Canyon. As they approached the Grand Canyon, the countryside was flat scrubland, permeated by isolated small cabins with flat bedded trucks, the cabins being homes of native American Indians. The opportunity came to pull up near a narrow crack in the flat scrubland, and look down a very deep and narrow canyon to the Colorado River. Next was the Grand Canyon itself, a truly spectacular sight, the family driving along the edge and parking up from time to time to look at a range of different views and to take pictures, before returning to Flagstaff for the night.

Checking the map out, Ken decided to go back via Four Corners, the plateau of Mesa Verde, Durango, Silverton, Ouray, Aspen and the Rockies to Denver. He was aware that he was on quite a tight schedule, since he needed to get back for the start of summer school. The route was via a windy state road that passed through the lands of a Navajo Indian reservation. "Can we stop for a wee, Dad," said Kerry, Ken pulling into an Indian Trading Post about two miles further on, alongside a cliff of huge stacked rounded rocks. There was a circle of some 20 Navajo sitting on the ground, blocking the way to an outside toilet. Ken, with some trepidation, approached the circle with Kerry, the Navajo graciously making way for them.

Four Corners was in a barren flat open area, a narrow dirt cul-de-sac leading to a succession of Navajo stalls and a very small number of Ute stalls, the Ute clearly much poorer than the Navajo. At the end of the track was a fancy tiled circle in the ground with two diameters at right-angles splitting the circle into four, the quadrants bearing the names Arizona, New Mexico, Utah and Colorado. There were very few tourists there but the family followed the lead of crouching down, putting hands in two of the quadrants and feet in the other two, so being able to claim that they had been in four states simultaneously!

They then drove to Mesa Verde, a narrow road leading to the top of the plateau. It was one of the highlights of their trip to see and climb down to the wonders of the cave dwellings in the steep sides of the vertical rock face of a valley. These dwellings had apparently only been discovered in the early 1900s. From the plateau, one could see the Rocky Mountains in the distance, the tops still being covered in snow in late May. Durango was a gem of a place, the family booking into a western style hotel with a balcony, the whole building being as if from a cowboy movie. Right outside the hotel was a classical western steam engine and railway that ran through the mountains to Silverton, a spectacular old mining town. "We need to push on, but it's a pity we cannot take the train," said Ken.

The family left after breakfast and stopped at Silverton for lunch. The restaurant had a chandelier and a long bar, behind which was a huge long mirror. Food was ordered from waitresses dressed in fishnet tights and costumes straight from the western movies. It was then off for a long drive and overnight stay in Aspen, Colorado. The next day, the family drove through Denver when suddenly in the town of Burlington, the voltage regulator on the car started to misbehave. Ken pulled into an auto repair shop where a mechanic claimed that the alternator was faulty but then broke it when he tried to change it. A new alternator had no effect, the mechanic not knowing what else to do. Ken went to a second auto repair shop and explained the problem, the mechanic there checking the battery to reveal that one cell was faulty. A new battery resolved the problem but Ken had lost several hours, the family driving off and eventually pulling into a rest area for food and gas. There they found the air completely still, the owner of the gas station saying that a tornado was reported to be nearby and that the family should shelter. They eventually set off again and drove through the night to get to Ken's class on time. After driving through Kansas City in the very early hours, they arrived back in Champaign Urbana, collected the course text and schedule, Carol then dropping Ken off at Altgeld Hall with some fifteen minutes to spare.

The summer school classes went well, Ken teaching from 8:00 a.m. to 10:00 a.m. and returning home for breakfast. Carol's mother and father, Joe and Floss, arrived in mid-July to stay with them, having flown with the entrepreneurial British Company, Laker Airways, to Toronto and taken a connecting flight with American Airlines to Chicago where Ken picked them up. The five of them planned a road trip out west to San Francisco, via Yellowstone National Park, returning via Medicine Hat, Alberta, to Toronto. However the news came through that Laker Airways were in difficulties and that Joe and Floss's flight had been brought forward four days. This was disappointing and they reconsidered their plan, Ken insisting that they did at least make Medicine Hat on the East side of the Rockies, this being the town where Joe had trained in World War II as a fighter pilot, flying Spitfires and Hurricanes.

Joe and Floss were both strongly family oriented, and they made every effort to meet all the needs of their large family. Joe had risen to be Deputy Headmaster of a local primary school but his efforts to achieve a Headship seemed to get blocked at every turn, Joe then continually blaming his current Headmaster, who he felt was totally inept. In the meantime he supplemented the family income by driving taxis for a cricketing friend and garage owner, Terry, in his spare time. One day he needed to take a child at the school to hospital and called in at Terry's garage for petrol. He was not aware that he was seen doing this by a member of the Educational Authority who reported that he was moonlighting in school time. It was this false observation placed secretly on the record that had led Joe to be repeatedly rejected, no doubt strengthened by the lack of support from his own Headmaster. Joe knew nothing of this, Ken only finding out years later from his Uncle Joe, who had been the first Mayor of the newly constituted town of West Bromwich and who discovered what had gone on. This travesty was further accentuated by the enormous contribution Joe made outside the classroom, including running the local branch of the Soldiers, Sailors and Air Force Association, which gave assistance to ex-forces personnel and their families who had come across hard times. He was also a volunteer reader for the blind. Floss herself also contributed to the community, being an excellent seamstress and teaching part-time evening and afternoon classes in the subject in local schools and colleges.

Following the end of summer school, Carol and Ken sent a number of large packages to their home in Ireland via surface mail. The five of them then put four cases into the huge boot of the Dodge Dart and prepared to set off for a final trip in mid-August. Their first target was De Moines, Iowa, the group arriving there in the dark and pulling into a very up-market hotel. Their rooms had balconies overlooking the swimming pool, an Orchestra playing alongside the pool and dining room. "Gee," said Ken to Carol, "I hope Joe and Floss don't expect this every night!"

The next day brought the expectations on accommodation down, the group staying in a roadside motel in two cabins, but with a swimming pool, this being surrounded by a dirt yard. Their aim now was Mount Rushmore in South Dakota, the group marvelling at the majesty of the Badlands with their white cliffs. Mount Rushmore was also spectacular with the four Presidents' heads being gigantic and the area below it underdeveloped, apart from a restaurant and tourist shop. Travelling next into Wyoming through Powder Pass Canyon in the Rockies, and through Ten Sleep (wondering where this name originated from) expectations again arose when the group stayed the night in West Yellowstone, a small pretty town with an old west feel to it. Following breakfast, they travelled into Yellowstone Park, the highlight of which was of course the geyser "Old Faithful". The crowd around it applauded enthusiastically as the steamy water rose majestically and on schedule into the air. Travelling north through the park, the group passed a large number of hot springs, many bubbling with hot mud and then headed towards the Gallatin Valley, Montana.

As they made their way through Montana, Ken noticed a helicopter standing on a pad alongside the road in open country. It was advertising rides at $7 per person, Ken saying "let's give it a go, who would like to try it?" The ladies all declined, Ken and Joe climbing in alongside the pilot. The experience was one of sitting on a chair that suddenly takes off but the ride was exhilarating as the helicopter swooped down into rocky ravines.

The Dodge crossed the border into Canada at a place called Sweet Grass, the group then staying overnight in Lethbridge, Alberta. Ken was sorry that the time did not allow a visit to Calgary but prioritized instead the visit to Medicine Hat. It was a hot day there when the car pulled into the cemetery, Joe being very moved as he visited the beautifully tended graves of young comrades who had died there in WWII whilst learning to fly.

And so the journey back to Toronto began, the group passing through Alberta, Saskatchewan and Manitoba, the road running in very long straight stretches alongside the Canadian Pacific Railway line. After an overnight stay in Winnipeg, the group entered Ontario, the journey becoming quite tiresome as the road made its way through continuous forests, with occasional views of small lakes. The schedule allowed a visit and overnight stay at Niagara Falls. "Soup or Juice," the waitress said to Floss at brunch the next day. "Yes please," said Floss, the waitress looking perplexed. The group laughed when they realized Floss had understood the waitress to say "Super Juice".

The family said their goodbyes to Floss and Joe at Toronto Airport and then started on the journey to Marlborough, Connecticut, where they were to meet up with Dennie and Peggy Malone and stay for two days with Pearl and Louis, Peggy's parents. The journey out west and back across Canada had been light on traffic, Ken grossly underestimating the time it would take, particularly on the New York Expressway, to get to southern Massachusetts. They were met at 2:00 a.m. by Dennie and Peggy with Kerry fast asleep and Carol and Ken struggling to stay awake. Carol made her way next afternoon to Barabault Jewellers, where Louis specialized in watch repair, and bought a very nice Bulova watch as a present for Ken. Soon it was time for goodbyes and the family drove into New York City, aiming to stop at a Howard Johnson's hotel, just off the Van

Wyck Expressway and close to Kennedy Airport. Unfortunately they missed their turn, panicking a little as they entered the airport. However they soon located the hotel on turning back along the Van Wyck. Carol and Kerry made their way to their room, Ken holding back to ask the desk clerk if he knew how he might get rid of his Dodge Dart and that he was looking for $100 as the price. "My daughter might be interested," the Clerk said, "I will call her." She arrived in 15 minutes, asked Ken about the vehicle's history and he gave her a ride around the local streets. "Yes, I'll take it," she said giving Ken the $100 on returning to her father's desk. He asked Ken if he could leave the plates on, offering him an additional $5. (Ken did wonder a few weeks later if it was all a con and if the car might be used for illegal purposes!) Ken went up to the room saying to Carol's amazement "I've sold the car!"

The family had two clear days in New York City before their flight home and did the usual tourist trips of going to the top of the Empire State Building, visiting Broadway, visiting the United Nations where they saw some moon rock, and taking a coach trip around the City. The latter caused Ken a scare when the tourists alighted from the bus in Chinatown. Ken was held up for 2 minutes and lost sight of them all, the bus also having left. Fortunately he managed to catch up with them! They also took a boat from Battery Park, on the southern tip of Manhattan, to the Statue of Liberty. Ken and Kerry wanted to climb the metallic spiral staircase to the library in the head of the statue, Carol refraining. Off they went, only to find that the temperature rose rapidly as they climbed the steps and so much so that Ken abandoned the idea.

The flight back to Dublin was uneventful, the family then taking the train to Belfast and a taxi to their home in Carryduff. They had rented their home to a PhD Physics student, his wife and child, the home now being empty. They were surprised to find wiring and electrical equipment in the garage, wondering of course if it had been used for terrorist purposes! But it transpired that the kit was all part of the PhD student's experimental requirements.

Chapter 9 Queen's and the Continuing Troubles

Life at Queen's was enhanced for Ken by the presence of Prof Maddox. However the year was very unsettling due to Carol having a miscarriage, the escalation of *the Troubles,* comparisons with the peace and family prosperity whilst at Illinois, and the unpopularity of Prof Maddox with certain members of the Department's staff, one of whom was openly hostile.

Ken was often given a lift into Queen's by Seamus, a trainee Architect, whose family were the only Catholic family in Ken's little cul-de-sac. Seamus's neighbours were the Arbuthnots, the father of whom was a policeman who had apparently been murdered by the IRA. A relative of Seamus had been interred by the Government in Long Kesh. Northern Ireland did however offer some respite from *the Troubles* through friendly neighbours (Kerry having a close friend in Kathy who lived next door) and through squash, football and cricket. The family also formed a close friendship with Ken's colleague Dr Roland Walker, his wife Jean and children Christopher and Julian as well as with Dr Mike Holcombe and his wife Jill, a biology teacher. Roland was an ardent fan of Manchester City, the real Manchester team as Roland would say, whilst Michael was a devotee of Crystal Palace.

Ken was a reasonably good squash player and was soon top of the ladder of those who played in the Department, apart from Dr Ken Glass, who did not participate. "Why don't you give Ken Glass a game?" said Roland, "I hear he is pretty good." A game was duly arranged and Ken was already changed and waiting for Dr Glass at the splendid Queen's facilities of some 10 courts. Dr Glass arrived but surprised Ken by entering the court wearing long trousers and a pullover! No wonder, he took Ken apart in three sets without breaking sweat!

The sports complex at Queen's also included five a side football, the Pure Maths team doing well in the inter-Faculty league. This then led to a challenge from the Mathematics students for an 11-a-side outdoor game. What the students did not know was that, whilst neither played 5-a-side, Prof Maddox had been on the books of Stoke City, whilst Dr McCartan had played in the Irish League. A brutal match followed, never to be repeated, the staff team winning 2-0.

During the early Spring Ken was offered the chance to join the indoor cricket nets with the YMCA team, who played in the Irish Senior League. Come the actual season, he found the wickets to be relatively slow, due to the damp climate, but he did well and was asked to open the batting and to keep wicket. He never made a 100 but came particularly close on two occasions. Once he was 75 not out without giving a chance, when the heavens opened and the umpires abandoned the match. In another game, YMCA were chasing a total of 190 and were 147 for 8 with Ken on 44 not out, having gone in at number 4. With just four overs now to go he proceeded to keep pulling the ball to the legside boundary in the gloomy light with the object of taking 11 runs an over. He took 33 off the first three overs, much to the frustration of the bowlers, some balls being pulled from wide of the off stump. He then took a big cut at the first ball of the final over, only to see it go deep to the boundary and be caught at third man!

Whilst sport gave some respite from *the Troubles*, the situation continued to be a great cause for concern. When the summer exams at Queen's came around, Ken and other Pure Mathematics colleagues were again asked to help organize and invigilate in the great Examinations Hall at the side of the main building. The duties involved many different but simultaneous exam papers, with several hundred students present, the complexity attracting additional pay of £2 an hour! On one occasion, when Ken was Chief Invigilator, an army officer and a university administrator came to him and informed him that information had been received saying that bombs had been placed in the Hall. Ken followed procedures, saying from the front: "Please stop and cover your scripts and papers. We have a security issue so an invigilator will lead each row out in turn to the lawns. Please do not communicate with any other student, we hope to return to the Hall very shortly. Thank you." It was remarkable how co-operative and calm the students were as they left and as a team of soldiers searched the building. After about 30 minutes the all clear was given and the students returned and completed their exams.

The period May 15th to May 24th 1974 saw the "Loyalist Strike" in operation, this leading to the cessation of transport services and the closure of petrol stations. Ken had one more session as Chief Invigilator to complete, both sides of the political divide permitting Queen's to continue their examinations. Ken had bought a Mark II Ford Cortina on his return from the States but was concerned that he had insufficient petrol. The journey to Queen's was quite alarming, a barricade having been erected across the main road in Carryduff, but he was let through by the loyalists on showing his Queen's ID and the paperwork giving the reason for his journey. Agricultural vehicles were spread across the lanes at various intervals and Ken's seemed to be the only vehicle on the road. He was very glad to get back safely without incident and without running out of petrol.

Following the usual summer work on Northern Ireland high school GCE marking, he again joined the family for a short break in England. Whilst on the boat journey across the Irish Sea, he suddenly had the thought that he had left the front door of his house open. He managed to call neighbours after docking and they confirmed he had indeed not pulled the door shut! Incidentally, one feature of the home was a corridor on entry that turned left at right angles after the staircase. The door to the home was clear glass and so Ken and Carol had a full length mirror fitted facing the door, this allowing them to check who was ringing the bell.

It was late in the Autumn term of 1974 that they decided that *the Troubles* showed no sign of receding and that it seemed best to try and move back to England. Kerry had started school at Carryduff and it bothered them that she seemed to show signs of beginning to be drawn into a sectarian education. Roland and Jean had come to the same conclusion but both Ken and Roland were aware that university openings in their fields were few and far between. Ken had also been reflecting on the future of life as a pure mathematician at Queen's; was he to spend his career teaching mathematics to mathematicians who would teach mathematics? At Illinois he had been exposed to teaching electrical engineers and the connections of engineering with Functional Analysis (essentially the theory of input-output systems) seemed to offer real opportunities.

Another concern was the reaction to what Roland, Mike, and Ken had done with regard to Level 0 Pure Mathematics teaching at Queen's. Numbers in the subject had been declining and the threesome came to the conclusion that the entire approach needed to be reviewed and the course made more student friendly and fit for purpose, the vast majority of the students not majoring in mathematics. The threesome were accused by some of the diehards of lowering standards and warned that the result would be a further decline. However the approach was well received by academic staff outside of the Department, numbers on the course rising dramatically! Prof Maddox kept his powder dry, declaring neither way, the trio always wondering how he felt.

Ken approached Prof Maddox to act as a referee should the occasion arise and this he kindly agreed to. An advertisement appeared late in the academic year for a position as Senior Lecturer in Mathematics at Sheffield Polytechnic, an institution that had long operated degrees and higher degrees and had an international reputation in Metallurgy. Ken applied, Prof Maddox expressing surprise, reminding him of his previously declared ambition of teaching in an English university. He received an invitation for an interview at Sheffield, the process to run over two days. There was a short list of some 10 applicants, Ken being informed at the briefing that only one of the two posts advertised was currently available and not the one he had applied for! Nevertheless he was asked to continue, candidates being shown around the Polytechnic and then briefed that they would have round-robin interviews with small panels the next day, including a short lecture, the topic to be drawn randomly from a list the next morning. A final short list would then be decided on and those chosen would go forward to a Polytechnic-wide interview.

Ken's interviews went well, the main issue to those asking questions being how and whether he could lower his teaching to the level of non-specialists. He drew a talk on introducing derivatives, his experience of teaching calculus at Illinois and in the Level 0 course at Queen's being enormously helpful. Following lunch, it was announced that four applicants would go forward to final interview, Ken being included. Again the final interview went very well, Ken also drawing on his work experience as a Wages Clerk, Railway Porter, Bus Conductor, Factory line worker and Steel Erector to draw out his ability to work with and understand people. At the conclusion of the interviews, the four candidates sat outside as the panel deliberated. The Head of Mathematics and Statistics, Dr Warren Gilchrist, eventually appeared and called Ken back in. As he entered, the Chairman, the Reverend Dr George Tolley, told Dr Gilchrist he had brought in the wrong person, Ken then being ushered out and the successful candidate Dr Steve Humble being called in. This was not to be the last time that Dr Gilchrist mistook Ken for Steve! Dr Gilchrist then took Ken into a separate room and explained that the panel wished him to be appointed to the second advertised position, but that it could not be offered until the person leaving handed in his official notice! Two weeks later he received a telephone call from a Personnel Officer at Sheffield Polytechnic offering him the post. "Will a salary of £6000 per year be acceptable to you Dr Jukes?" said the Officer. Ken reeled back in shock since his salary at Queen's was only £1700 per year. "Yes, I think so," he stammered. "A formal written offer and contract will be sent immediately," concluded the Officer. It transpired that the salaries of polytechnic academic staff and, later, university academic staff rose substantially and in line between 1975 and 1976. Ken immediately called home with the good and startling news. As had happened on leaving Wales for Belfast, Carol again became pregnant!

Roland also received good news; he had widened his search to include the possibility of secondary school teaching and was offered a position in Leeds. (Roland went on to a hugely successful teaching career in Leeds, rising to the Headship of a major comprehensive school.) On receiving the offer, Roland tendered his resignation from Queen's, Prof Maddox winning the fight for the vacancy to be re-allocated back to his Department. A serious issue then arose when Ken received confirmation of the post at Sheffield and tendered his own resignation, the date being beyond the normal date by which resignations had to be given. Prof Maddox, again fighting for jobs in his Department, and fearing non-replacement, apparently initially refused Ken's resignation. Ken naturally felt aggrieved and wrote to the Vice Chancellor, Sir Arthur Vick, who wrote a very kind reply giving him permission to leave at the end of August. Indeed, Queen's and Sheffield were very generous, resolving a problem with the FSSU Pension scheme of the University being non-transferable to the Teachers' Pension Scheme that all Polytechnics ascribed to. There was another Universities Scheme, USS, which did align with the Teachers' Pension Scheme, the Bursar at Queen's agreeing with Sheffield Education Authority to loan Ken to the Polytechnic for two months at his new salary, whilst they transferred his pension credit from FSSU to USS to Teachers!

In order to achieve the Pension transfer, he was required to visit the Education Offices at the Town Hall in Sheffield and to sign various papers. He duly travelled to Sheffield and was directed down a long corridor to the office of the Pensions Administrator. The meeting took just over an hour, Ken then leaving the office and walking along the corridor, only to find it blocked by a wall consisting of a huge array of flowers. He went to the edge, pushed his way through and was immediately jumped upon by security officers, who were even more perturbed to find he was from Belfast. It transpired that the Queen was visiting Sheffield on that day, her schedule including a stop at the Town Hall!

Ken and Carol approached local Estate Agents and put their Carryduff home up for sale at a price of £10,000. Just seven days later a single man in his 20's visited the property and made an offer of £10,000 which they immediately accepted, their outstanding mortgage being £6,600. They then journeyed to Sheffield to seek out possible housing and schooling. Ken had been thinking of a new mortgage allowing purchase of a house in the £12,000 region but were advised at Royal Insurance in Sheffield to work on a factor of 2.5 times salary and so to consider properties around £18,000. They looked around the Sheffield area and came upon a new build, about to start, of 12 detached houses in a quiet cul-de-sac, Walton Close, just off the Holmesfield Road in Dronfield Woodhouse. They were very taken by the size of the houses, the view, the separate garage and carport and the proximity of a primary school within walking distance.

Chapter 10 Sheffield and British Steel

It was summer 1975 when the family moved back, Kerry staying with Floss and Joe whilst Ken and Carol went to Sheffield and signed up for the first house to be built in Walton Close. It was planned to be completed within 6 months, they thus having to find rented accommodation initially. This proved to be difficult until they located a large old three storey furnished house in the beautiful Peak District village of Tideswell, Derbyshire, just 18 miles from Sheffield. Unfortunately there was no central heating, even though the house was owned by a plumber in the village, and neither Carol nor Ken realized just how cold the house would be in the winter. It all seemed perfect in the warmth of the summer. They were also able to find a storage location in the village for their furniture when it arrived from Ireland. Another bonus was that Kerry was accepted into the village Primary School, within walking distance of their home. A final bonus was the welcome given by neighbours David and Glenys Hughes, who had two children, Samantha and Daniel, of Kerry's age and who quickly made friends. Ken was able to drive in good time across the moors, via Curbar Edge, to Sheffield and he thoroughly enjoyed the beautiful scenery.

He made his first visit to Sheffield Polytechnic before the start of term to set up office accommodation but particularly to find out his teaching timetable. The Department of Mathematics and Statistics was located in Herriot House, directly opposite the central bus and railway stations and alongside the Post Office sorting building. Stepping out of the lift on the fourth floor of Heriott House, he was alarmed to see a large but youngish man sitting on top of a youth and holding a hammer threatening him. The Department Secretary appeared and said the police were on their way. It transpired that the youth had been caught breaking into the cash box on the public telephone on that floor!

Ken was informed by the Department Secretary that he was to share an office on the second floor with Dr John Stone and that he should see the Timetabling Officer, Dr Peter Hempson, about his timetable.

He had previously been informed that his schedule would include the "MSC" course and took this to mean a Master of Science level course, only to be taken aback later to find that it stood for HND (Higher National Diploma) in Mathematics, Statistics and Computing. The huge use of acronyms was his first experience of a significant difference in the culture of universities versus polytechnics. A second was the huge difference of teaching hours between university and polytechnic staff; he had typically taught 6 formal teaching hours per week in university (9 hours per week at Illinois) but was now to teach 18 hours per week in the polytechnic. Another challenge was that the courses were mainly integrated courses of mathematics, statistics and computing, these being in the "service" of other Departments, Ken's courses covering HND and Degree work in the home Department, Mechanical Engineering, Civil Engineering, and Biology. The computing element also included use of the Polytechnic's IBM mainframe to teach programming in Fortran and Basic. "How am I to cover this," he thought, his officemate Dr J.A.R. Stone (did his father have a sense of humour?) being enormously helpful and kind and guiding him through his first year. John pointed out the availability of evening classes in programming which Ken availed himself of and knew exactly what and why his students the next day had such questions since he himself had faced the same issues the night before! Somehow he survived thanks to John and other colleagues, but he did wonder if he had been put through an initiation exercise on his first day of teaching.

The first class was to be held on the fourth floor of a five storey building, accessed by walking through the bus station. He got there 5 minutes early, only to find men in the room working on re-painting it. A notice on the board read: "Dr Jukes, please go to room 814 in the 12 storey block," Ken rushing to the adjoining building and taking the lift. Room 814 was a men's toilet and a note on the door said "Dr Jukes, please go to Room 312 in the 10 storey block!" This lay opposite the main road and adjacent to the railway station, Ken now running there and arriving 10 minutes late! Fortunately the students were still there, waiting patiently and the day went well thereafter. No-one owned up and Ken was left to reflect on whether disorganization was a feature of polytechnics or was he the victim of a set-up?

It was in week three that Ken was asked by Mr Dick Eddowes, a senior and highly respected member of the Mathematics staff, if he would take on a special task of tutoring an exchange student from the University of Frankfurt, who needed to take a course in Functional Analysis, Dick knowing that Ken had taught this at Queen's. It was suggested that Ken would be paid the standard overtime rates and he readily agreed. Heidi was a beautiful and very intelligent girl but her English was very weak as was Ken's German, yet somehow they survived by following Prof Maddox's textbook "Elements of Functional Analysis" and using a German/English dictionary. Ken noticed after two months that he had not been paid overtime and went to see his Head of Department. Dr Gilchrist was normally a quiet and very polite man, but he must have had a bad day since he immediately told Ken rather brusquely, "No we are not going to pay you, but you must carry on!" So he did and was rewarded at the end of the year with the gift from Heidi of a very nice stein carrying the University of Frankfurt emblem.

Ken had not counted on the type of weather on the moors outside of Sheffield, his days being lengthened by the dense fog on occasions over the top of the moors on the way to Curbar Edge. However, Christmas soon came and went and it was on January 23rd that Carol had yet another anti-natal visit to Jessop's, the Teaching Hospital in Sheffield. She was told that it was going well but would be at least another two weeks before the baby came. Snow and ice had settled into the Peak District by this time but the roads were still passable. It was about 10:00 p.m. that evening that Carol began to feel pain and so, given the previous miscarriage, they decided to play safe and call an ambulance. The roads had become treacherous by now but the ambulance duly appeared and, again as a matter of precaution, took Carol away to Jessop's Hospital in Sheffield. Kerry joined Ken in bed and they proceeded to sleep, waking about 8:00 a.m. the next morning, Glenys banging on the back door. "How can you still be asleep?" said Glenys, "we have been trying to get you up for ages. Carol had her baby, a boy, at about 3:00 in the morning. Both are doing well." Ken was very pleased and surprised. "Ahh, he will qualify to play for cricket for Yorkshire, having been born in the county!" he said.

As the end of lease date on the rented property approached, Carol and Ken started to become concerned whether their new home would be built in time, their worst fears being borne out when they checked progress and found that the downstairs ceilings had dropped in the middle, the builder explaining that the joiner had not fitted the supporting batons correctly and that the ceilings would need to be taken down, redone and replastered. There would now be a delay of two months, requiring them and now 2 children to find alternative accommodation. Assistance arrived via an offer from an antique dealers, the Pennocks, in Tideswell who had a very small flat available above their shop and living quarters. They also invited the family to join them in their TV lounge on weekends. The family somehow managed to survive in the tiny flat, the pressure being relieved by Glenys and David who constantly invited them down to their cottage.

The builder finally gave the family clearance in June to move into their new home in Dronfield Woodhouse. It seemed absolutely enormous after the stifling space in the flat, the new house having a large 23 feet by 12 feet lounge, the 12 feet widening to 17 feet half way along at the point where the open oak staircase descended into the lounge. There was a 13 feet square kitchen with a hatch to a small dining room. The house also included an entrance hall off which lay a downstairs loo and washbasin. The three bedrooms and bathroom upstairs were all of a very good size, the rear views from which stretched many miles in the distance towards Rotherham. The front and rear gardens were enhanced by additional space on the side of the home and the garage and carport were all of a good size. All this and to their great joy, gas central heating!

Ken spent much of the summer enhancing the exterior. He built a patio with a low fancy stone wall across the rear of the house and with an opening and steps to what would be the lawn. Flower beds were built at the front and rear and a vegetable garden was designed at the bottom of the garden, where they planted peas, potatoes and runner beans. As winter approached they discovered that the west facing carport acted as a wind tunnel, the wind off the moors being so strong at times that it blew out the pilot light via the exhaust fitted at the side of the kitchen. Ken saw the builder and arranged for one of his men to put a garage door on the front of the carport and to close in the rear and to include a window and door. What a difference the huge salary increase and the savings from the year in Illinois had made!

In the following Spring Ken was asked by the builder, Mr Smith, if he would be interested in giving his nine year old son Tom, some tutoring in Mathematics. He was already tutoring two teenage girls, the Goodchilds, who lived in a large detached house beyond the fence at the bottom of the garden. During the weekend, Ken designed a wall and gate to run along two sides of the trapezoidal area of their land, from the back of the carport to the back of the house. The wall was to be 6 feet high and of fancy patterned 9 inch by 9 inch blocks, and the trapezoidal area, the path alongside the carport wall and the rear patio were to be paved with 3 feet by 2 feet paving slabs. Ken built the fancy wall and then started laying the slabs alongside the carport wall leaving a 2 feet gap for a flower border. However with the path being above the level of the floor of the carport, the aftermath of rainfall led to a seepage of water through the carport wall. This was solved by taking out a line of cement pointing from the carport wall, just above the soil level, and inserting damp course material in the line, bending it also to give a protective shield along the base of the wall and well below the carport floor level.

Ken focussed with Tom one day on multiplication and its application to area and volume. It transpired that with all the building going on, a delivery of house bricks had been received that day, each rectangular block being bound with steel ribbon. Ken discussed with Tom how he could find how many bricks were in a block, the two of them then going out to measure the length, width and depth of a single brick and then multiplying the three numbers to give the volume of the brick. They then went out again and measured the length, width and height of one of the large rectangular blocks to find its volume. Tom then divided the volume of the single brick into the volume of the large block to find how many bricks there were in the large rectangular block. Finally Tom multiplied by the number of rectangular blocks to get the total number of bricks.

That evening Tom explained to his father what they had been doing in the lesson and showed his father the results. "What!" exclaimed Mr Smith, "they have delivered a lot less bricks than they have claimed for!" The next day Mr Smith called in to thank Ken and, seeing he was laying slabs, said "Take as much building sand as you need." Ken took him at his word and over the next two weeks laid some 169 slabs in 3 inches of sand!

It was during the following academic year that two events at the Polytechnic occurred that would have a significant impact on Ken's career. He had been given the chance to tutor a class in the Electrical Engineering Department, the level of their mathematics being relatively high. In doing so he came into contact with Mike Grimble, a Control Engineer and PhD, recruited from General Electric in Rugby, who was running a research seminar group in his Department. Ken was invited to attend and was astonished to find that the audience and speakers included academics from Cambridge University, Imperial College London, Sheffield University and from British Steel's national Research and Development Centre, the so-called Swinden Laboratories, near Rotherham. Further, the participants were also using functional analysis in their research and so Ken, with his subject knowledge and work experience in engineering, felt totally at home and with a good understanding of the talks. This led to a fruitful friendship and interaction with Mike who was producing research publications at an enormous rate. Mike would often ask Ken to check the mathematical accuracy of the content, leading him to being mentioned and thanked in several publications. Mike was backed up very strongly by his wife Wendy, and seemed to have enormous energy, Ken sometimes being awakened after midnight by the sound of the letterbox as Mike dropped his latest draft research paper through for Ken to look at.

Mike had an unusual background having attended a secondary modern school and having no national GCS O-levels or A-levels. Indeed he was trained as an electrician and one day he picked up a mathematics book at his library and discovered he could understand quite a lot of it. He used to read whilst sometimes at the top of a ladder in his factory in Grimsby and became known as the "Prof". His academic skill was recognised and he did an HNC at Grimsby Technical College, an Honours degree at Rugby College and an MSc and PhD at Birmingham University. He also completed a part-time BA in Mathematics with the Open University! When later on Mike secured a Chair (Professorship) in the old universities, Ken amused himself with the thought that Mike might be the only electrician to have achieved such a change in class from Electrician to Professor!

Midway through his second academic year at Sheffield, Dr Gilchrist suggested to Ken that he might like to be considered for an industrial secondment. Mike Grimble was at the time supervising a couple of PhD students who were addressing the problem of the design of an automatic control system for the Szendzimir Rolling Mills, British Steel having several such mills in the various works in the area. Discussion with the manager Mike Foster at British Steel led to an agreement for Ken to be seconded to Swinden Labs, Rotherham for the next academic year. The secondment would include working on the Szendzimir project and various other projects around Sheffield and so Ken needed transport, taking his automatic Ford Consul with him. British Steel paid travel expenses within trips to various works but not to and from Swinden Labs. At the time bus fares in the Sheffield area were subsidized, there being a flat rate of 10 pence per journey, the Polytechnic only covering the bus fares and so the substantial British Steel travel expenses were very welcome to Ken.

The first job at British Steel was laboratory based and involved the mathematical modelling of arc furnaces, there being some 43 parameters involved. Although being aware of principal component analysis, Ken had little faith in the model and seemingly upset the lead engineer for the project by suggesting that there was little hope of controlling all such parameters. He then started work on the control system design for the 20-high Szendzimir Rolling Mills, working with the lead British Steel engineer for the project, Ken Dutton. There were six of these mills in one works alone in Sheffield, each mill costing some $15,000,000, the mills having being been designed on a laboratory scale in the USA, and then scaled up, a Scandinavian firm designing the physical control system. The mills were used in Sheffield for the rolling of cold stainless steel. Mike Grimble's two PhD students were working on aspects of modelling and control system design since there was apparently no known mathematical model of the full industrial system. At the same time, Ken Dutton was developing a mathematical model using "Hetenyi's theory of beams on an elastic foundation" and writing subroutines in Fortran to represent different software models of aspects of the various features of the mill. However during the year, given contraction of the steel industry and demand for control engineers from many outside sources, the original 12 control engineers in the Department at Swinden labs dwindled to just 4. One result of this was that Ken was also called upon to assist Ken Dutton with factory trials of other control systems.

One such system involved an issue with the arc furnaces and the quality of scrap metal. Occasionally dealers would increase the apparent weight of scrap by including concrete inside barrels. One of the aims of the arc furnace was to reduce carbon content, but the three massive graphite electrodes would bear down on such barrels due to the poor conductivity and might ping like a tuning fork and snap, the pot of molten steel now having pure carbon in it! A crane would then have to be used to extract the broken section of the electrode from the pot of molten steel. The aim of the development project was to introduce a computer control system that would detect non-conductivity and stop the electrode assembly bearing down on the concrete.

Another project led to several visits to a major melting shop containing a set of three arc furnaces in a row, each handling some 160 tons of molten steel, the pots being moved by overhead cranes running on a track high up in the shop. The idea was to automate the process of pouring the molten steel to create steel ingots. At present the 160 tons of molten steel was swung across by a crane to a train of flat-bed railway trucks, each truck containing six cases that reminded Ken of six Egyptian mummy cases. The bottom of the pot had two overlapping metal plates, called flowgates, controlled pneumatically by the teeming crew, the plates each having a circular hole, the overlapping of which controlled the flow of molten steel into a case. The rate of flow could be viewed from a weighing device hanging from the crane but of course as the level of molten steel in the pot decreased, the size of the overlap of the flowgates would need to be increased to maintain the rate of flow into the case, this affecting the nature of the steel.

When a set of six cases had been completed the train pulled forward so the next truck could be serviced. At the end of the process the train pulled behind the service bay and at a set time, the cases were lifted off, each ingot revealing a red hot block. No wonder the two Kens had to wear fibre glass protective clothing and helmets. They also had a screen to hide behind to provide additional cover from the enormous heat. It was like facing 10,000 electric fires!

Engineer Dutton had designed a computer control system varying the rate of flow of molten steel, this replacing the hydraulic system and eventually the jobs of the teeming crew. It was quite understandable that the crew did not cooperate with them. Another problem was the nature of the overall operation; if one wanted a certain type of steel and the resulting metallurgy went wrong (samples of the steel in the pot were taken from time to time and analyzed immediately in a lab), then it was normal to pour lead into the furnace, creating a softer so called free-running steel that was easier to work with and easier to sell. The more complex steel required greater control of the teeming process, Ken spending many hours sitting in his car in the snow waiting for a mix that would give a good trial of the proposed control system.

The time came when Engineer Dutton got the nod about the complex quality of the steel to be teemed and sent Ken up the huge flights of metal stairs to the crane in order to plug the new system into an outlet in the box section of the crane. He entered into the box section below the crane controller's cabin and immediately started hopping about, the heat starting to melt his shoes. He managed to get some wood sections to stand on, plug the system in and then had to drop the cable down through live buzz bars to Engineer Dutton on the bay. All very dangerous but part of the difficulty of development testing. The system test was then carried out successfully.

Travel to and from Swinden Labs could be extremely difficult in the snow, Ken deciding to walk there on one particular day, the snow being very deep and whipped up into drifts by the wind from the moors. As he passed the corner at the top of Mickley Lane, walking on the snow above the height of the field hedges bordering the road, a snow plough went into the snow bank crunching into two cars hidden underneath the drift, there fortunately being no-one in them. On another day, he had real difficulty driving back in the Consul and decided to take the main road through the town of Dronfield. Cars had been abandoned on the hill to Dronfield Woodhouse but Ken managed to keep going by zig zagging and allowing the car to back into the kerbside snow bank from time to time. Suddenly a double decker bus appeared further up the hill, the driver leaning out and shouting "move out of the way, the bus is sliding!" It slid past the Consul, slamming instead into a vehicle abandoned in the snow.

With the reduction in the number of British Steel engineers and his work on helping model the Szendzimir Mills, Ken was asked to be a second supervisor of Engineer Dutton's part time PhD. This ran over the next five years, Ken Dutton eventually securing his PhD, his chief oral examiner being Prof Neil Munroe of UMIST. As Ken explained to the interviewing panel, Engineer Dutton's thesis was extremely long since it seemed important that the thesis contained not only the mathematical model of the Szendzimir system but also the proposed control system design, thus improving the credibility of Mr Dutton as a practicing Engineer.

Chapter 11 Back to Academia

Ken had now completed his secondment but the link with British Steel continued through the Szendzimir project and PhD supervision. He also continued to develop interests in applications of mathematical modelling and to publish in journals, sometimes with one or more of Dr Harry Gretton, Dr Mike Grimble, Dr Graham Raggett and Dr Peter Hempson. It was around this time that he was approached by his neighbour and friend, Keith Goodchild, for some advice about spreadsheets, the content of which Ken was sworn to secrecy. Keith was a very senior figure in British Steel and had been charged with looking at the redistribution of the manufacture of steel products in England and Wales, with a view to closing down some of the plants. It was quite a harrowing task looking at all sorts of "what if" scenarios, some of which impacted on and led to a plant closure in the Black Country.

With the increasing costs of petrol, the Consul with its 17 miles per gallon became prohibitive to run. Carol and Ken decided to try and sell it and advertised in the Sheffield Telegraph. To their astonishment they immediately sold it for the asking price! The reason? Their buyer was a man in his sixties with a wooden leg who needed both the driver space the Consul afforded and an automatic car! Ken then bought the worst car he had ever had, a fairly new Austin Allegro, that Kerry called a space-mobile. Whenever you turned a corner, the wheels screamed as if the brakes were locked on (they were not) and the acceleration was pathetic. He sold the car within six months in part-exchange at a dealers for a yellow Ford Escort and was so relieved to get rid of the Allegro.

One of the aspects of academic life at Sheffield that Ken enjoyed was the emphasis on sandwich (co-operative) courses, both the thin (six month) and thick (12 month) models of supervised paid employment in relative industrial/commercial/medical/government organizations being in operation. Besides visits to students, Ken was given the opportunity to work with the Industrial Training Co-ordinator, Malcolm Brewer, in setting up the positions. On one occasion, Ken found himself in a meeting with the Chief Employment Officer at a government institution, the person being the father of Jim Stanton, one of Ken's fellow students and close friends at the University of Wales. Jim had briefed his father about Ken who said at the end of their talk about openings: "Dr Jukes, I could take six students and so would you select them and send me their CVs." "Certainly Sir," said Ken being both elated and concerned since it was very rare to secure more than two openings and how could he be sure that the six would be good enough and maintain his reputation!

Another visit was to the Royal Naval Establishment in Greenwich, the sandwich student, Greg, assisting in training on software packages, the students being Naval officers of various ranks and ages. Greg was a black student with a great personality and was qualified in the martial arts. Ken discovered that apart from his role in software support, Greg was leading and training groups in the martial arts in the Naval Establishment. Ken was hosted for lunch with Greg and an Officer in the wonderful dining room, with its classical painted ceilings. "I say Sir, pass the salt to port please," said an elderly Officer on the long table a short distance away. What was very noticeable was that Greg was the only black face Ken had seen throughout the visit but they were then served dessert by a young black waitress who eyed Greg with total admiration.

It was during the following year that the senior position of Industrial Training Officer in the Department was advertised, Malcolm having been promoted to a position in the central administration. Ken applied, was shortlisted and interviewed but was unsuccessful, feedback from Dr Gilchrist being that he was deemed to be too valuable as an academic and researcher. Ken felt quite hurt since he had thought long and hard about whether to apply and felt it unsatisfactory that his career direction was being made for him. However it then transpired that Dr Gilchrist announced that the Department was to be split formally into two sections, with Dr Gilchrist in overall charge but supported by a Head of Mathematics and a Head of Statistics & Operational Research. Ken was encouraged to apply for the Head of Mathematics and received wonderful support from the staff in Mathematics and from senior staff in the management of the Polytechnic! He was successful and started his new role in April 1980. However, it transpired that after several years wait for an operation for varicose veins, he was called into the Northern General Hospital and had a major vein removed. A fine start to his new role!

Ken was a regular snooker player with Peter Hempson and Graham Raggett, all three being members of the Millhouses Bowling and Tennis Club, a private concern with four tables in a well-kept building for snooker, opposite the Robin Hood public house. Graham had achieved breaks in excess of 50 and was a class above Peter who himself was much better than Ken. They operated a handicap system that varied after each game. All three entered the Polytechnic wide snooker competition, Ken being embarrassed when they all got through to the semi-finals. "So this is what the new Head of Mathematics and his staff do," was a regular quip in the Common Room! In the quarter final Ken, given his problem with colour blindness, asked the referee to let him know if he was aiming for the brown rather than a red. "Foul," said the referee as he played the brown rather than a red. "I asked you to tell me," said Ken! "Oh, I thought you were joking," said the referee. Ken settled himself and somehow managed to win on the pink ball.

It was during the autumn when Ken visited the Cheshire Homes in Totley, Sheffield, Carol having secured a part-time job there. The Homes had been initially set up by a World War II hero and veteran, Captain Sir Leonard Cheshire VC, and provided residential places and support to disabled people. One man, Brian, had essentially lost the use of his hands in that he could not keep his wrists up but he could move his fingers. Another lady, Gillian, was wheelchair bound and had no use of her hands. Carol had asked whether there was any possibility of a trip by the residents to the Polytechnic's computer laboratories in Heriot House. A trip was duly arranged and even though the Polytechnic was still in the age of dumb terminals linked to mainframes, the games available still gave some enjoyment. Gillian was able to participate using a stick held in her mouth and became quite good at controlling its movement to press the keys. Ken in the meantime had designed a keyboard with a wide built-in rest at the front and had it made in aluminium by technicians in the Mechanical Engineering Department. The keyboard had magnetic legs to attach to the keyboard of the dumb terminal and its holes had also been enlarged and smoothed so that Brian could support his wrists on the rest and press the keys by putting fingers through the holes. It took some time for Brian to achieve single presses but he went on to master the keyboard and later to pursue his ambition of writing a book.

One of Ken's aspirations for the Mathematics Department was to develop its own degree program. While it had a degree equivalent course, validated by the Institute of Mathematics & its Applications, topping up the 2-year HND, almost all of its teaching was in the service area. This was not the case with Statistics which had an established Honours Degree, nor for example Computer Science which had all levels of courses. One reason for Ken's view was the high quality of the Mathematics staff, with 23 of the 25 having PhDs and many of them being active and publishing in various journals. An opening came up through the enormous help of the internally powerful Head of the Department of Computer Science, the Reverend Ian Draffan, (who enjoyed both a pint and a smoke) who supported the inclusion of a Mathematics route within the Combined Honours Degree Programme. Ken and Dr Alan Northcliffe worked on this during the academic year 1981-82 and were supported by other academic Departments who gave a few student numbers each from their own programmes to allow the new stream to begin.

It was early in 1982 that Ken, amazed by Mike Grimble's enormous publications output, suggested to him that he ought to consider applying for university Chairs in Control or Electrical Engineering. Two such openings came up quickly at The Royal Military College, Shrivenham, and Strathclyde University, Mike being interviewed for both and securing a chair at Strathclyde. Ken also noticed an advertised position of Head of Department of Computer Studies & Mathematics at Bristol Polytechnic, the city of Bristol always having an attraction to him. He applied and was offered the position there, a new chapter in his career and *another story*.

About the Author:

Ken Jukes is a native of Tipton in the Black Country of England. He was 4th in a family of 8 children and the first in his extended family to go to university where he gained First Class Honours and a PhD in Mathematics. He was on the faculty of the University of Wales, Queen's University, the University of Illinois, the Open University, Head of the Department of Mathematics at Sheffield Hallam University, and Professor and Dean of Science, Engineering, Mathematics and Statistics at the University of the West of England, Bristol. Besides extensive project experience in industry, commerce and government institutions, he has published in international journals and books across Mathematics, Control Engineering, Computer Science, Management and Teaching. Ken was a part-time inspector for the quality of university teaching in both computing and mathematics and chaired the UK Committee of Professors of Mathematics and Computing. He is a Professor Emeritus, Fellow of the Institute of Mathematics & its Applications, a Chartered Mathematician and a former Chartered Engineer and Member of the British Computer Society. He is also a qualified teacher grades 6 to 12 in Mathematics with Gifted Endorsement in Florida where he taught high school at Pine View, Sarasota, Florida for 5 years.

Printed in Great Britain
by Amazon